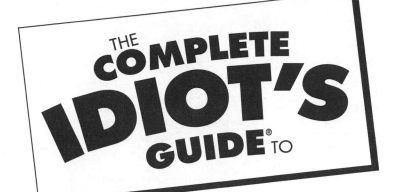

THE COMPLETE IDIOT'S GUIDE® TO

Scrapbooking

Illustrated

Second Edition

by Wendy Smedley

ALPHA

A Pearson Education Company

International Standard Book Number: 0-02-864372-0
Library of Congress Catalog Card Number: 2002113269

04   8   7   6   5   4

Interpretation of the printing code: The rightmost number of the first series of numbers is the year of the book's printing; the rightmost number of the second series of numbers is the number of the book's printing. For example, a printing code of 02-1 shows that the first printing occurred in 2002.

Printed in the United States of America

Note: This publication contains the opinions and ideas of its author. It is intended to provide helpful and informative material on the subject matter covered. It is sold with the understanding that the author and publisher are not engaged in rendering professional services in the book. If the reader requires personal assistance or advice, a competent professional should be consulted.

The author and publisher specifically disclaim any responsibility for any liability, loss, or risk, personal or otherwise, which is incurred as a consequence, directly or indirectly, of the use and application of any of the contents of this book.

For marketing and publicity, please call: 317-581-3722

The publisher offers discounts on this book when ordered in quantity for bulk purchases and special sales.

For sales within the United States, please contact: Corporate and Government Sales, 1-800-382-3419 or corpsales@pearsontechgroup.com

Outside the United States, please contact: International Sales, 317-581-3793 or international@pearsontechgroup.com

Publisher: *Marie Butler-Knight*
Product Manager: *Phil Kitchel*
Managing Editor: *Jennifer Chisholm*
Senior Acquisitions Editor: *Randy Ladenheim-Gil*
Development Editor: *Michael Thomas*
Senior Production Editor: *Christy Wagner*
Copy Editor: *Cari Luna*
Illustrator: *Chris Eliopoulos*
Cover/Book Designer: *Trina Wurst*
Indexer: *Julie Bess*
Layout/Proofreading: *Angela Calvert, John Etchison, Kelly Maish, Trina Wurst*

Contents at a Glance

Contents

Foreword

I still remember the first time I walked into a scrapbooking store. I wasn't a complete beginner—I'd created scrapbooks as a teenager—but what I saw both astounded and scared me. I loved the piles of paper, rolls of stickers, shelves of albums, and machines for die cutting. What I didn't love was the instant anxiety attack. "Oh no," I moaned. "Where do I begin? I don't want to look stupid." I timidly approached a clerk, who guided me to just the supplies I needed. I felt so grateful, but also like a complete idiot.

I signed up for a couple scrapbooking classes, where I copied every technique and used only the supplies demonstrated by the instructors. Soon, I was ready to see what I could do on my own, and before long, I was addicted to scrapbooking. Today, it's not only my favorite hobby but my business as well. Still, I'll never forget the anxiety I suffered when starting, and hundreds of scrapbookers have told me they've felt the same way. Just hearing words and phrases like "lignin-free," "acid-free," and "journaling" can scare away even the most enthusiastic novice.

If you're a beginner, you could be saying, "This whole scrapbooking thing is a lot more involved than I expected. I thought it was supposed to be fun." It is! Scrapbooking is one of the most enjoyable, worthwhile hobbies out there. You're making memories for yourself and your family that will last for years. Imagine how delighted someone in the future will be that you took the time and made the effort.

But making these memories takes motivation, preparation, and information. You've already got the motivation or you wouldn't be reading this book. Next comes the planning. The problem lies in not knowing which archival products to buy, how to use them, and how to make them last. That's where *The Complete Idiot's Guide to Scrapbooking Illustrated*, now in its second edition, comes in handy. Here you'll find everything you need to get started and keep going—especially if you're struggling.

If you're beyond the beginning stage, you know it's tough to keep up on all the new techniques and products. Or maybe you've hit a creative block—we all do—and just need something to give you a jump-start or jolt to help you create a masterpiece. If that's where you find yourself, *The Complete Idiot's Guide to Scrapbooking Illustrated, Second Edition*, can help you review not only products, but themes, tips, and ideas as well. If you're like me, you can never get enough!

Scrapbooking today is about more than construction paper and edible paste. It's about using the right products to create long-lasting pages your family will treasure. It's about taking memorable photos. It's about writing down your memories—even if you think you have the worst handwriting in the world.

The Complete Idiot's Guide to Scrapbooking Illustrated, Second Edition, offers guidance for scrappers on any level. Use it to look up products, terms, or themes. You'll be able to walk into any scrapbook store with confidence. Better yet, you'll be able to create scrapbook pages that will stand the test of time. You can also help your loved ones preserve their own memories, too. I've found this as rewarding as preserving my own. Here's to smart scrapbooking!

Lisa Bearnson
editor, *Creating Keepsakes* magazine

Introduction

Are you embarrassed by all the photos you have crammed into shoeboxes over the years? Do you cringe when your children ask what their first word was, because you can't remember it? I experienced all these moments, as have many others. That's why people like me have turned to scrapbooking as a way to record our lives. Preserving history for the future and creating family unity (not to mention providing a much-needed creative outlet) is what this craft is all about.

Scrapbooking is enjoyed by thousands of people and spans age, race, culture, and taste. You will find something that works for your lifestyle needs and be thrilled with the results. So begin this journey with open eyes and remember that something recorded is better than nothing recorded. Set aside some time once a week, once a month, or even once a year to record your history. We all have a story to tell. Some choose to tell their story using pictures and only a few words. Others choose to use many words—they write about the photographs and mementos and how they feel about the depicted image. Some like to focus on family, while others love to make interesting books about special events, travel, or pets. Something scrapbookers have in common is the enjoyment derived from browsing through completed albums and remembering the days gone by.

It is important that you tell your family's story, but don't forget yourself. As you read, make notes in the margins on projects and pages you want to do. If inspiration suddenly hits you while you are reading, then be sure and make a note to include it in your next scrapbook.

How to Use This Book

To teach the craft of scrapbooking in an easy and organized fashion, the book is divided into six parts. **Part 1, "Putting All the Puzzle Pieces Together,"** covers scrapbooking for the newcomer. Maybe you are totally new to scrapbooking and have no idea what it is, or you have an idea or a few punches, and you want to know more. Start here to get a taste of the beginnings of this hobby, learn what items are essential, and find suggestions for shopping.

Part 2, "Setting Up Shop," is a guide to the vast array of products available to you, not only products for the general crafter, but also archival supplies that are made specifically for scrapbooking. I'll tell you my favorite ways to use these products, such as decorative paper, pre-illustrated accents, pens, and cutting tools, and give you numerous ideas to get you started. After reading this part you will have the confidence you need to wander into a scrapbook store, virtual or real.

Part 3, "Essential Skills to Complete Those Albums," will help you with essential skills needed to get the most out of your scrapbooking. You'll get ideas on how to organize your scrapbook workspace so that it is compatible with your scrapper needs. It also has sections on organizing the treasures you've unearthed during your hunt for photos, and suggestions on how to include these in your scrapbook. You will read about organizing your photos whether you have one shoe box or an entire roomful. Photography tips for the scrapper will also be helpful for you to read when selecting film or a new camera. You will also read about how you can include text in your scrapbook and document through words your photo story.

Part 4, "Scrap It, Stick It, Store It," will give you the skills to move beyond basic scrapbooking to become a more creative scrapper. You will learn some basic color rules to help when selecting your colors for scrapbooking. What scrapbooking style best describes you? This question will be answered for you as you look at the different types of scrapbooking styles. Learn some basic design rules for scrapbooking that will help you complete pages in no time at all. Last, but not least, you'll find information on building your own scrapbooking community—how to find one that fits your needs and keeps you motivated.

In **Part 5, "Great Pages for All Ages,"** you will get tips on how to turn your scrapbooking into a specific book, from a theme book to a nonevent album that would communicate a feeling or tradition. Look here for how to get your kids started preserving their memories alongside you. Teach them archival methods while they are young.

Part 6, "Post-Grad Scrapping," gives you a window into the latest mixed media trend. You will read descriptions of a variety of popular mixed media, see layouts showing how they an be used, and get tips on where to purchase these items. Thanks to scrapjazz.com you will get to see these elements used in a variety of styles. Take time to read how best to adhere these different mixed media in order to use them successfully in your scrapbook. You'll also find information on using traditional crafting methods, such as quilling, in your scrapbook.

Helpful Hints

This book contains four types of boxes that offer extra information about scrapbooking. Look for the following:

From the Archives

Here are interesting facts about scrap-booking, such as how fast the industry has grown, facts about people in the industry, and general fun tidbits. These are for your reading pleasure.

Shortcuts

Shortcuts are tips and tricks to save you time. They are things I have learned through the years I have been scrap-booking and teaching.

Sticky Points

These are warnings and places where you could get stuck and even stopped. Read these points to keep moving ahead. Learn from the mistakes I have made and seen others make—I want to save you grief.

Words for Posterity

Every hobby has its own set of terms and lingo—you will learn scrapbook-ing terms by reading these boxes. With these words under your belt, you'll be able to walk into the scrapbooking world with confidence.

Acknowledgments

The summer of 1996 found me searching for a small break from my taxing duties as a mom of four young children, which led me to a part-time job as a weekend cashier in a local scrapbooking store. Since then I have dabbled in a variety of positions in this industry from business owner to teacher to magazine contributor. I want to acknowledge and thank those who have helped along the way to teach and instruct me. I ask endless questions and appreciate those that have spoken freely with me, too many to list.

I have gotten to understand and appreciate the role the owners of independent scrapbook retail stores play in the industry and I want to acknowledge their hard work and dedication to the industry. Without them working all those hours, we wouldn't have as many products available to us.

I appreciate and acknowledge the talented and dedicated staff of Alpha Books working on this project with me, especially Randy Landenheim-Gil for giving me the opportunity to update this book and bring you a second edition.

Acknowledgments also go out to the industry manufacturers who have spoken with me and so freely shared their knowledge and products with me. Keep cranking out all those great new products.

A thank you goes again to Yvette Dyer for supplying the line art for this project!

It has been a pleasure working with Andrea Steed of Scrapjazz.com and all of her talented team of designers—thanks for contributing your talent to the last part of the book—you guys are great!!

I would also like to acknowledge and give thanks to the team behind *Creating Keepsakes* and *Simple Scrapbooks* for motivating me and thousands of other scrapbookers—keep up the good work!

My appreciation goes out to my family and friends who have supported and encouraged me through this process—my parents for teaching me the value of hard work, my younger brother Shawn for demonstrating how to change, to my sister Laurie for lending me her ear on my many projects and giving me advice and help, my other sister Heather for her words of encouragement and her generosity, and to my older brother for giving me cause to reflect and connect to those I love. I would also like to thank my in-laws for their love and encouragement that never seems to run out!

And finally my husband and children who give me reason to scrapbook—thanks to my husband Kent for his encouragement and his ability to make me laugh—I love you! To my five sons whose zest for life keeps me going. I love to photograph them and document their changing lives—I am truly blessed to have you as my sons!

Trademarks

All terms mentioned in this book that are known to be or are suspected of being trademarks or service marks have been appropriately capitalized. Alpha Books and Pearson Education, Inc., cannot attest to the accuracy of this information. Use of a term in this book should not be regarded as affecting the validity of any trademark or service mark.

In This Part

Part 1

Putting All the Puzzle Pieces Together

It's a common misconception that you have to be an artist to scrapbook. "I love scrapbooks," my friend Teri told me, "but they never turn out the way I want them to. I guess I'm just not artistic enough." The truth is, anyone with the right tools can create a beautiful, one-of-a-kind scrapbook!

In this part, I'll introduce you to the trend of scrapbooking and explain why it's so popular. Why do people do it? How did it begin? What do you have to have to start? Let's begin this journey together.

In This Chapter

◆ Tap your creative juices by scrapbooking (and you don't have to be an artist)

◆ Scrapbooks help us remember the past, keep us connected with family—and lead to cleaner closets!

◆ Kids and family members will have fun making scrapbooks together

What Is Scrapbooking, Anyway?

The urge to collect and display mementos is something all people have, and people have been making scrapbooks for ages. With items such as scotch tape, rubber cement, and even flour paste, they compiled books and books of photographs to pass on to their families.

Your neighbors are doing it, the babysitter is consumed with it, even your daughter is asking for help doing it. Let's face it—we all know someone who scrapbooks. We're going to unravel the mystery of this hobby and teach you how to be an educated scrapper. In the last 12 years, scrapbooking has become even more popular. Some crafting experts predicted that scrapbooking would soon fizzle out, but they were wrong! With all of the new developments in the photography industry, more people are taking photos and wanting to enjoy the fruits of their efforts.

This chapter is all about scrapbooks—what they are and the reasons people enjoy this hobby. Whether you are a stay-at-home parent with a house full of kids, a single person living with roommates, or a newlywed with pets, read on to find out why scrapbooking is for you.

What's Your Story? Tell It with Scrapbooking

When guests visit my home, I love to show my latest scrapbooking pages. "Your books are so cute, but that's too much work," one of these visitors told me. It can be time-consuming if you let it, but frankly, if scrapbooking feels like work, you probably aren't using the right products. Scrapbooking is supposed to be a fun way to preserve photos, certificates, and other memorabilia.

Here is a delightful double-page layout capturing a
trip to Disneyland highlighting the various characters.

Words for Posterity _____

Modern **scrapbooks** are much more than photos and clippings. A scrapbook is an artfully arranged collection of photographs, memorabilia, and journaling (a fancy term used to describe any words you write in your book) that's fun to look at.

Most people who start scrapbooking quickly become passionate about it, filling more and more pages. As a scrapbooking teacher, I have taught many beginners and seen their enthusiasm grow. When I ask my students why they like to scrapbook, I get the same answers over and over: "Scrapbooking is my creative outlet. It's the one thing I do that is artistic." Or "I want to preserve my history." Or "I'm concerned about the erosion of the family unit. Scrapbooking is a way to keep my family connected."

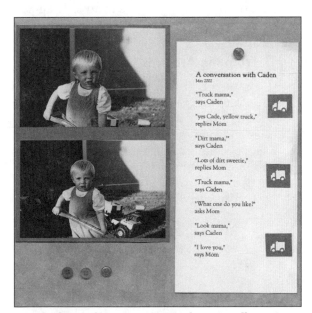

Note how the pictures and storytelling are combined to make a scrapbook page.

From the Archives _____

Hobby Industry Association is a New Jersey–based international trade association. The association was founded in 1940 and now has more than 4,000 member companies. Because all employees of a member company are members of HIA, the association is the world's largest in the craft and hobby industry, representing hundreds of thousands of industry members.

Preserving the Past

Until now, long-term storage methods weren't available for the average person. With all the recent technological advances, it's now possible for anyone to take up scrapbooking with a minimal investment of time and money. You can make a scrapbook as simple or elaborate as you like. But regardless of how much or how little you do, you are preserving a portion of history.

Shortcuts _____

Do you own your mother's wedding dress, your grandmother's quilt, or your great-uncle's cello? Try photographing it and writing the history behind it in your scrapbook. That way, even if the item is in storage, you can still display it.

Up a Tree—Researching Your Family History

If you aren't lucky enough to have information on your ancestors, help is out there. Many people have taken up *genealogy*, the study of the history of a family, and love it.

Why do we want to discover our ancestors? For some people, an interest in genealogy satisfies a desire to solve a mystery, and other people are interested in the medical history of their family. But most people who begin researching their roots simply want to know where they came from—the names of their ancestors, where they emigrated from, and what their lives were like. Most avid genealogists say that there is an excitement in learning about their heritage. Genealogy is the most researched topic on the Internet, and it is a task that consumes hundreds of thousands of people all over the world—you never know what you are going to find out when you start researching.

> ### Words for Posterity
>
> **Genealogy** is the study of the descent of a person, family, or group from an ancestor. Some people are interested simply in creating a family tree, and others delve deeply into the history and characters in their family's past. Either way, researching your family's history can be a fun and exciting project.

Begin the Climb

If you are interested in researching the history of your family, I suggest starting with your family tree (known technically as your pedigree chart). Take some time to jot down what you already know about your family. Start with the names of your siblings, parents, aunts, uncles, grandparents, and, if you know them, your great-grandparents.

After doing this, you may discover that you already know quite a bit about your family's history from stories that you've heard over the years and family heirlooms and keepsakes. Or you may find that there is a great deal to learn. Either way, discovering your roots can be a lot of fun. Remember to enjoy the journey and don't get too frustrated when you can't find that important record or name—learn what you can about your ancestors and record what you discover for others to enjoy someday. Who knows, maybe you'll discover you have some famous, or infamous, relatives from long ago!

> ### From the Archives
>
> Before people kept written records, the history of a family's genealogy was passed down orally. Without writing, communities and families relied on memory and, the *Encyclopedia Britannica* notes, they may have used mnemonic systems with knots or beads that indicated who people were, what position they held, and important events.

Branching Out

Try going to the library or bookstore and browsing through their books on the subject—bring some books home to learn the terms and lingo. You will find many books and online sites to get you started researching your family tree:

◆ A great Internet site with more than 47,000 links is www.cyndislinks.com.

◆ Another very good site to check out is www.familysearch.org—this one is so popular that within its first week, the providers had to upgrade it so more people could get access.

From the Archives

Coats of arms—symbols on shields depicting the wearer's identity in battle—were used dating back to twelfth-century Europe. They later served as a family's emblem and were often ornamented with helmets, wreaths, crests, and a motto.

All in the Family

We are living in an era of technology. It seems as though everyone has a personal computer, one or two cell phones, and a fax machine. Although technology has made our lives easier in many ways, it has also taken us away from our families. Keeping up with all this technology takes time, time that we used to spend as families. I think that scrapbooking's popularity is a response to that.

Of course, "family" means different things to different people. I have a husband and four sons, two cats, and a dog (not to mention some goldfish and my boys' latest bug collections).

I also have parents and siblings, as well as in-laws, aunts, uncles, and cousins. But a family unit can consist of a single parent and child, a grandparent and grandchild, roommates, a single person and a pet, or any other combination. It's important to maintain family unity in any circumstance. Scrapbooking is a great way to do this. Your scrapbook will reflect the things most important to you, and family is probably high on this list.

Sharing Family Memories

Scrapbooking is something I do that brings me closer to my children. I think it's important for their self-esteem for us to record their accomplishments. My kids love to look at their baby books and tell me who came to see them in the hospital. They take turns looking at their books and love to tell me all about who is in the photo (as if I wasn't there taking the pictures!). Kids gain a great deal of self-confidence when they see that their accomplishments are important enough to be documented in the family album.

Here is an example of a simplified family tree chart that is perfect to use in a scrapbook.

Sticky Points

Don't overlook the hard times in your scrapbook. Though they may be painful to document, they are still an important part of your life. Be discerning in selecting photos for your pages, though, and try to leave out photos that are disturbing or distasteful.

I know that even as an adult, I enjoy pulling out my baby books and going through them. It brings back all my childhood memories—good and bad. My favorite childhood photograph is the one of my brothers, sisters, and me in front of the Christmas tree. It was Christmas Eve, and we all had new pajamas. Everyone had big excited grins on their faces—except my older brother (10 years old at the time). It seems like he was a little embarrassed about the teddy bear jammies my mom gave him. So instead of a smile, he wore a smirk—and never wore those pajamas again! We teased him for years about that photo, and looking at it now, it brings back all my childhood memories.

As adults, we need to remember our roots from time to time. Since I had a happy childhood, I like to go through my albums. It reminds me of what it was like to be a child and teaches me how to treat my own kids. If your childhood was not a happy one, remembering can be a healing process and a way to remind you how far you've come. Whatever the case, creating a scrapbook at any point in your life will give you a surprising perspective.

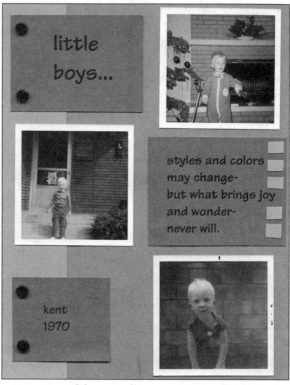

little boys...

styles and colors may change— but what brings joy and wonder— never will.

kent 1970

It's enjoyable to reflect on one's childhood when working on childhood layouts.

Words for Posterity

Memorabilia is certificates, documents, and other three-dimensional items that tell a story. Memorabilia can include souvenirs from trips, or mementos from special occasions or historical events.

Commemorating Family Events

Scrapbooks can also become a central place for family memorabilia. You can change junk and clutter into a family history. Instead of tucking certificates into boxes, I like to showcase them in my albums. That way I can look at them whenever I want (and my closets are a lot cleaner!).

✂ Shortcuts

> Is your bulletin board or refrigerator covered with announcements, drawings, and awards? Instead of tossing everything into the garbage, go through it once a month and save the best drawings. Even things like soccer schedules and party invitations give detail and personality to your scrapbook.

Don't forget the kids! Although we like to make scrapbooks for them, it's even more fun to give them some materials and let them go to work. Though their creations might not be polished-looking, they are priceless. Kids enjoy making scrapbooks for grandparents and friends, and what schoolteacher wouldn't love a scrapbook as a year-end gift?

I enjoy incorporating certificates and awards into the pages of our family scrapbook.

✂ Shortcuts

> If you are overwhelmed by the number of photos you have to work with, remember that you can simply use the extra-special ones. Be selective—you don't have to include every picture from the three rolls of film you took at Niagara Falls.

Also, scrapbooks are a great way to stay connected to extended family. If your family is like mine, you've got aunts, uncles, and cousins you rarely see. They may send you Christmas cards every year. Instead of stacking them in the corner or throwing them in the recycling bin, organize them with photos in a separate album. This is the same album you'll use to put photos of the family reunion in or other extended family events. This way, you can pull out the photo albums and teach your child who's who.

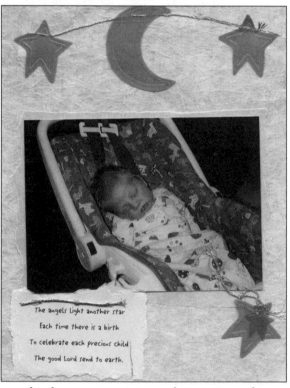

The angels light another star

Each time there is a birth

To celebrate each precious child

The good Lord send to earth.

This layout captures and preserves the emotion surrounded by the joy this baby brought along with him.

Shortcuts

Does the idea of compiling a family history seem overwhelming? Try this: Whenever your kids say something memorable, jot it down on your calendar. Now you've got some quotes to go on your scrapbook pages. This won't take much time, and you won't forget all the cute things your kids said.

Letting Your Creative Juices Flow

One reason people don't scrapbook is that they think they are not "artistic." Well, in my three years of teaching scrapbooking, I have not had one artist walk into my class, yet each participant has taken home art. That's because scrapbooking is a skill that is easily learned. There are so many products available today. All you have to do is learn to put them together!

My favorite subject in school was art. I remember the funny smell of the paste and the frustration of those blunt safety scissors. I also remember the joy of creating something beautiful (at least to my young eyes) from nothing more than paper, crayons, glue, and scissors. I enjoyed the process as much as the result.

From the Archives

People like scrapbooking so much that some hotels and spas offer scrapbooking retreats as a vacation package. One company offers traveling classes and a traveling store. There are even weekend retreats planned for scrapbooking. Check these websites for more information about scrapbooking trips:

www.highcountryretreats.com

www.momandmescrapbooks@aol.com

www.getawaygals.com

For most of us, creativity is a way to get away from it all. I know that when my twins were six months old and my older boys were three and four, creativity became a priority. I made it a point to get away and scrapbook once a week. It gave me great satisfaction. Not only was I able to take a break from my hectic family, I was creating something for that family. It isn't a matter of having enough time; it's a matter of making time for the things you like to do.

Sticky Points

Many people give up on scrapbooking before they start because they think it is too complicated. Continue through this book, and you will find the information you need to get started and feel competent.

Being creative brings self-confidence and satisfaction. Many people do it as a retreat from the hustle and bustle of everyday life. My friend Debbie is going through a rough patch right now, but she always makes time for scrapbooking. "Scrapbooking is my sanity," she declares. "With all the problems I'm having, it's the one thing I do that makes me feel productive." I know many people with similar feelings; no matter what's going on in their lives, they find time to scrapbook because they need to.

The Least You Need to Know

- Modern scrapbooks are much more than photos and clippings. A scrapbook is an artfully arranged collection of photographs, memorabilia, and journaling that's fun to look at.

- Anyone can create a beautiful scrapbook; make one that reflects who you are.

- Scrapbooking is a terrific creative outlet that helps preserve your family history.

- The world is moving faster all the time. Scrapbooking is a craft that can help you slow down, reflect, and spend time with family.

In This Chapter

◆ The beginnings of the scrapbooking industry

◆ Why we don't use those magnetic albums anymore

◆ Adapting museum storage techniques for your photos

Chapter 2

Scrapbooking Pioneers and Modern Methods

When was the last time you took a look at your old photo albums? I pulled out my magnetic photo albums 10 years ago, and the pictures were yellowing and faded. I tried to rip them out, but they were stuck! I swore I would never use that kind of album again, but, unsure of my options, I didn't know what to do. I knew that museums preserved artifacts in their storage vaults, but, unfortunately, I didn't have an entire museum at my disposal, and I'm laying odds you don't, either.

People have been compiling family histories for years in Bibles and other ways, but these original scrapbooks often fell apart, creating a need for archival products. If you are like most people, you have treasures to preserve, and while they might not be considered valuable to an outsider, they are irreplaceable to you. Luckily, a scrapbooking supply industry has sprung up over the last decade that allows the layperson to take advantage of museum storage and presentation techniques. After all, as a scrapbooker, you are just as interested in displaying your photographs as in preserving them.

So before you give up (or build onto your house!), read this chapter. Without turning your house into a museum, you can preserve your pictures and memorabilia while making them easy to view. This chapter gives some background on scrapbooking companies, the tremendous growth of the scrapbooking industry, and archival-quality products that you can find and use easily.

Scrapbooking Origins

Scrapbooks were probably first made during the Victorian era. Scrapbooks got their names because they were often made from scraps of cloth and printed paper that were collected and pasted into blank books. These books were looked upon the same way we would admire a stamp or coin collection today.

From the Archives

Many scrapbooking designs reflect an enduring fascination with the Victorian era. Decoupage, the art of decorating surfaces by applying cutouts and then covering them with varnish, was created during that time and is still done today.

When photography was invented more than 150 years ago, people began to compile photo albums, typically using photo corners to adhere them to pages of blank books. In the early years of photography, photographs were most often taken by professionals in a painstaking process. Because film speeds were very slow, people had to pose perfectly still as the camera made its exposure. As film technology progressed, film and cameras became more affordable, and it became common for people to own their own cameras and to collect pictures in albums.

People have also commonly kept journals, diaries, and personal notebooks. Through journals that my own pioneer ancestors kept, I have learned about their struggles and triumphs. Modern scrapbooks are a melding of personal journals, old scrapbooks, and photo albums into one. What is unfortunate about many of the first-person accounts our ancestors kept that have told us so much about life hundreds of years ago is that many of them are faded and crumbling. Many documents that have been invaluable in piecing together information about various historical eras have been lost, even books that were only put together a few decades ago. This is largely because the materials that people used deteriorated and did not stand the test of time.

First (Preservation) Steps

For a long time, it seemed that you could choose either to display your photographs by placing them in albums or to preserve them by packing them away in various storage containers. Now, because of some innovative companies, we have the techniques to do both.

Modern scrapbooking may have started with a Utah woman named Marielen W. Christensen, who put pictures, mementos, and journals together, though it is likely that others came up with the same idea around the same time. In 1987, two women, Cheryl Lightle and Rhonda Anderson, collaborated to begin a company called Creative Memories. This was the first company to offer photo-storage information and products directly to the consumer.

"Is Your Paper Lignin-Free?"

After a few scrapbook supply companies raised consumer awareness, other companies became inundated with calls regarding their products. Questions such as, "Is your paper *lignin*-free?" became commonplace. The craft industry responded tentatively at first with a few products and then made many more as demand increased. People wanted products that were not only safe for scrapbooking, but attractive, too!

Many of the companies that responded were already established in the crafting industry. They made products for rubber stamping and paper crafting. They improved their products to make them appropriate for scrapbookers.

Words for Posterity

Lignin is a substance in paper that breaks down to become acidic over time. Paper with lignin is not suitable for archival projects.

You know a crafting trend has reached major proportions when it has its own magazine, and there are currently several devoted to scrapbooking. Lisa Bearnson started *Creating Keepsakes* with Don Lambson in 1996, and it played a big part in connecting manufacturers with retailers and consumers with products. Another magazine, *Memory Makers*, was created around the same time by Michelle Gerbrandt. These magazines provide you with some great ideas for your scrapbooks, and really keep you up to date with the industry. You might want to pick one up at your local newsstand or even become a subscriber. Now there are numerous publications dedicated to the scrapbook hobbyist.

On the heels of the big corporations were many cottage industries. Unlike the big companies that had all sorts of resources, these were companies that were created by people who saw a need and filled it. Most of these self-starters became successful by specializing in one aspect of scrapbooking. One small company was started by two women working on their scrapbooks who thought an oval-shape cutter would make their work easier. They teamed up to develop a special tool called the *oval cropper*.

Words for Posterity

Oval croppers cut paper and photographs into oval shapes. After you determine the size of the oval by moving the blade, you position the cropper on the item to be cut and trim all the way around.

Scrapbooking has come a long way from gluing bits of photographs to paper, and one of the unique things about this craft is how it has been driven by the interests and needs of the people who enjoy it.

Keeping It All Safe and Sound

All the new scrapping supplies have one thing in common: They safely preserve photographs and other mementos. According to the American Institute of Conservation, preservation is defined as "the protection of cultural property through activities that minimize chemical and physical deterioration and damage and that prevent loss of informational content. The primary goal of preservation is to prolong the existence of cultural property."

Words for Posterity

Archival is a term describing an item that is considered safe for photos and long-lasting.

Modern scrapbooking became *archival* scrapbooking when the pioneers in the industry adapted museum techniques to home preservation. Scrapbookers are indebted to this industry for all the guidelines we now have. Since technical books on archiving are a little complicated for the average person and museum storage spaces are a little big for the average apartment, it's fortunate that *conservationists* have done all the important research for us. More than the average scrapbooker, conservationists make a career of preserving memorabilia, spending years learning how to restore and care for precious treasures from the past; we have learned a great deal from them.

Words for Posterity

A **conservationist** is someone who makes a career of preserving artifacts, artworks, or precious documents. Most museums employ conservationists to look after their works of art.

Museum conservators go to great lengths to protect priceless works of art from damage. Museums take strict measures against damage by light, pests, temperature, humidity, air pollution, and dust. Temperatures are controlled 24 hours a day with humidistatically controlled heating, ventilating, and air conditioning. Special light fixtures are installed to minimize damage by ultraviolet radiation, and because water damage is a major concern, museums are equipped with water alarms.

Sticky Points

Remember those magnetic photo albums that have the sticky backs and the clear plastic sheet that covers the pictures? Do not use these books as photo or scrapbook albums—the adhesive used contains acid and emits chemicals that damage your photos.

To keep photos and other paper items in good shape, museums store them in acid-free envelopes or sandwiched between acid-free paper in metal boxes, and most of the photos are matted with acid-free mats. Of course, photographs that are stored this way are rarely viewed, and when they are, it is mostly for research.

That's nice, you're thinking, but what does all this have to do with me? I'm not a professional, and I don't work in a museum. I just want to save a few photos. Obviously, family photos don't lend themselves to such rigorous methods because they are meant to be looked at and enjoyed—imagine your 12-year-old asking for a baby picture to take to school and you refusing to let him because your family photos are *encapsulated* in metal boxes! Thankfully, archival techniques have been adapted to suit everyday purposes.

Words for Posterity

Encapsulation is the process by which a document or photo is surrounded by material to completely protect it from the elements.

As scrapbookers, we are concerned with three things: photo-safe quality products, storage for supplies and completed books, and accessibility to our photographs.

Stamp of Approval

Initially, products available for archival scrapbooking were acid-free white or cream cardstock and black felt-tip pens. To satisfy the demand for more options—and more attractive options—companies introduced new products. Almost overnight there were so many new papers, stickers, and markers, it was hard to know which were truly safe. To simplify the process of looking for archival-quality materials without mastering museum-standard conservation requirements, the Creating Keepsakes company created a program called *CK OK*, a stamp of approval that says the items are okay to be used in scrapbooks. Manufacturers of scrapbooking and craft supplies apply for the seal and submit their products for testing. If the product passes, the manufacturer can carry the CK OK seal of approval. This makes it a lot easier for scrapbookers to know what they are purchasing.

Shortcuts

Look for the "CK OK" mark on products you buy for your scrapbook. These supplies have been tested and determined to be safe and long-lasting.

Smart Storage

Even when you use good archival products, how you store your scrapbooks and photographs is important. These items are sensitive, but with a few simple precautions, they will be around for a long time. Here are a few things to keep in mind when storing your scrapbooks.

Sticky Points

Try to wash your hands and have others wash theirs before handling photos; this prevents a lot of dirt and oil from being transferred to your pictures.

- Moisture distorts and damages photos. If you have water-damaged photos, take them to a professional photo restorer.

- Acid causes paper to break down. Many kinds of paper (newspaper, for example) are highly acidic and need special treatment before being used in a scrapbook.

- The oils that are present in your skin are damaging to photos. Always handle photographs by their edges or copy the professionals and wear cotton gloves when handling your photos.

◆ Photographs can be damaged by temperature fluctuations, so keep your scrapbooks in a place where the temperature is fairly consistent, preferably around 75 degrees. Avoid storing scrapbooks in areas with high humidity, such as a basement or attic.

◆ Not only does sunlight fade photos, it discolors cardstock and stickers. Storing your scrapbooks in a dark place is a good idea, and remember to close your scrapbook when you're done looking at it.

Easy Access

The third most important concern for scrappers, after protection, is accessibility. My friend Susan told me that she had worked on a scrapbook for a year. It was a masterpiece, she said, but she was afraid to let her kids look at it. I had to convince her that scrapbooks are made to be looked at. The way to protect the photographs and other items in your book is to make sure that protective materials are used throughout. As safe as you want to keep the stuff in your book, there's no use going to all that work if you can't look at them when Grandpa comes over.

Shortcuts _____

Kids can get a load of fingerprints on page protectors. To clean them, mist a paper towel with a little of your favorite window cleaner and wipe. The shine will return.

When handling photographs, use a product known as Hands Off—it's an acid-neutralizing lotion or soap.

Before they make it into a scrapbook, it's good to organize photos and store them in a photo-safe storage box. (These come in all sorts of cute decorator colors now.) It's also a terrific idea to duplicate photos and send them to faraway friends and relatives. With all the new technology, photos can now be sent through e-mail, as well as the good old-fashioned way. Nothing thrills grandparents like receiving pictures in the mail that they can start bragging about to their friends and neighbors.

Leaps and Bounds

What started out as a kitchen table craft has grown to huge proportions. Families everywhere are enjoying the fruits of the scrapbooking laborer as they reminisce over last year's vacation or connect to their ancestry. Most states have numerous stores dedicated to selling products to the scrapbooker. People all over the world are getting bitten by the scrapbooking bug. Canada has close to 100 stores; the United Kingdom and Australia are getting involved as well. There are also a couple of scrapbook shows, and many hobby and craft shows have scrapbooking segments. You can even buy products on QVC. I am excited to see what the next three years will bring in this industry.

Modern scrapbookers are holding parties that people are calling modern quilting bees—people getting together for social interaction, while creating a lasting heirloom. Scrapbooking is definitely here to stay.

The Least You Need to Know

- Scrapbooking has a long history, stretching back to the Victorian era, and the industry has taken off dramatically in the last three years.
- These days, anyone can get archival products that will preserve your photographs and mementos.
- Many magazines and books are available for interested scrappers.
- The three most important issues for scrappers: archival quality of products used, good storage for supplies and completed books, and accessibility.

In This Chapter

◆ Talking the talk—terms for the beginner

◆ How to begin organizing your scrapbooking essentials (without breaking your bank)

◆ Choosing adhesives, writing tools, and protectors

◆ Cardstock—the kind of paper you absolutely must have

Absolute Scrapbooking Essentials

Okay, you're convinced you want to scrapbook, and you've developed those dozen rolls of film that had been sitting in your kitchen drawer since last summer. You can't wait to put them into albums and show everyone your creative accomplishments. What now? Before you head out the door ready to buy, buy, buy, slow down and take stock of what you really need.

If you have an unlimited budget, you can go to the store and buy whatever you like without regard to cost. But if you're like me, you need to be careful with your money. This chapter tells you what you absolutely must have to start a beautiful scrapbook and defines the scrapbooking terms with which you should be familiar.

Scrapbookese: Terms Every Beginner Should Know

If you were to spend an afternoon with fly-fishing fanatics, you would most likely miss much of their conversation. Like many other hobbyists, scrapbookers have their own lingo. The first time I walked into a scrapbook store, I heard so many new terms that I was lost in five minutes. To help you seem like a pro before you have even mounted your first photo, here is a compilation of basic scrapbooking terms you will need to know before you go shopping.

◆ **Acid.** A chemically reactive substance often found in paper that fades photographs. Products that are acid-free help you preserve your photos and other paper mementos.

◆ **pH level.** This tells you how acidic or basic something is. For scrapbooking, you want to use products that are low in acid and have a pH level of 7 or above.

- **PVC (polyvinyl chloride).** All you need to know about this is that it is harmful to photographs. You should use products that are composed of polypropylene in your scrapbooks.

- **Polypropylene, polyethylene, and polyester.** Stable plastics that are safe for photos. Look for these names on labels of products you purchase for scrapbooks.

- **Lignin.** A naturally occurring substance in wood that can break down into acids over time. Lignin must be removed from the paper to make it last. An example of what lignin does is the yellowing of newsprint. Newsprint is low-quality paper that contains high levels of acid, as well as lignin. If you leave newsprint exposed to the sun for a few days, you can see how lignin breaks down into acids because it discolors and becomes brittle.

- **Acid migration.** When an item that is acidic comes in contact with another item that is less acidic, the acid can transfer over. This happens when acid from paper, dirty skin, or any item comes in contact with other items, and the acid transfers over.

- **Buffered.** A term used to describe products that are capable of maintaining the basicity of a solution; in other words, use buffered paper to neutralize acids that migrate from a photo to paper.

- **Archival.** A designation for products and techniques that will prevent your photos and important documents from fading, deteriorating, and yellowing over time.

- **P.A.T. (Photo Activity Test).** A test created by the American National Standards Institute that determines whether a product will damage photos. If a product passes the P.A.T., it is considered archival quality and safe to use with your photographs.

Sticky Points

You can't always tell if paper is acid-free by the label, so ask a store clerk for information. Many scrapbooking stores have policies regarding acid-free paper and will go so far as to guarantee that all their paper is acid-free, lignin-free, and buffered. So go ahead and ask!

Shortcuts

Why not start a scrapbooking club? If you don't have a store nearby where you can take classes, and you know some people who like to scrap, start meeting together at home or at your local library, or rent a place to meet. Some scrapbooking groups charge monthly dues that are used to buy new products everyone can use.

- **Reversible adhesives.** These adhesives can be unstuck. Reversible adhesives are desirable if you think you might ever want to move an item in your scrapbook to some other place.

- **CK OK.** Designation given by a company called Creative Keepsakes; CK OK is the scrapbooking industry's equivalent to the Good Housekeeping Seal of Approval.

From the Archives

In order to clarify the scrapbooking industry's standard terminology, the CK OK team has written a book called *Saving Our Scrapbooks*, which has an industry-standard glossary.

If you need more details on these terms, check out Appendix B for a list of books. To make sure you feel completely confident in the company of hard-core scrapbookers, you're going to have to learn the following lingo. Do this and you'll really be able to "talk the talk."

◆ **Crop.** (1) To cut or trim a photo. (2) A gathering of scrapbookers working on album pages and sharing ideas with each other.

◆ **Workshop.** A class in scrapbooking usually held at a store and taught by an expert. Participants bring photos and pages to work on and get advice from the instructor.

◆ **Page exchanges.** These are fun activities in which participants are invited to create a page to share with up to 10 other scrapbookers. Sometimes a theme is given, such as a holiday like Halloween. Each participant at a page exchange brings enough copies of an original page to trade with the others and goes home with as many different pages as there are members, as well as the inspiration of their fellow scrapbookers.

◆ **Product swap.** If you've got duplicates of products, such as paper or stickers, or some tools that you don't use anymore, such as decorative scissors or paper edgers, gather them together and call some friends. Ask them to bring their unwanted scrapbooking items to trade. After it's done, you've got a clean closet and tons of new products—free!

◆ **Scrapbooking club.** Any group of scrapbookers that meet regularly to encourage each other and compare books. Their main goal is to scrapbook together and share products.

◆ **"Pass the chocolate."** A phrase commonly spoken by members of a scrapbooking club.

◆ **Layout.** Grouping of pages in your scrapbook that go together. Most often this is composed of two pages that lie side by side with the same theme.

Shortcuts

Use a pH testing pen to test the acidic level of paper products. The pen mark changes colors depending on the level of acid present.

Now that you know some of the technical terms and the jargon, you won't be confused when you go into a scrapbook store, open a scrapbooking magazine, or go to an online scrapbook chat room.

Last is a list of scrapbooking terms that might mean different things to different people. Here is what they mean when I use them in this book:

Wendy's Lingo

◆ **Mount.** What you do to your photo when you stick it on another piece of paper.

Words for Posterity

An **adhesive** is any substance that is used to make items stick to each other—glue, paste, tape, reversible adhesives, and so on.

◆ **Double mount.** To stick two pieces of paper together and adhere a photo to the top paper. This is similar to layered mattes in framing.

◆ **Accent.** This catch-all phrase refers to stickers, die-cuts, and other decorative elements that you add to your page.

◆ **Heading.** The title on a page.

◆ **Title page.** The page at the beginning of a scrapbook or section, such as "Smedley Family Reunion, July 1999" or "Kwaanza at Keisha's, December 1995."

◆ **Theme.** The overall focus of the scrapbook, such as a Family Vacations album.

◆ **Wendy's Wonder List.** Throughout this book, you will find lists of my original scrapbook ideas and favorite uses for products. Feel free to adapt them to your own scrapbooks.

◆ **Page.** The bare paper that is the foundation of the scrapbook decorated with photographs, embellishments, and journaling.

◆ **Memorabilia.** Items other than photographs that can be included in your scrapbook, such as documents, certificates, artwork, and souvenirs.

◆ **Mixed media.** Three-dimensional accents such as brads, eyelets, and fiber that are used in scrapbooking.

Shortcuts

Photo corners are a great way to get photos on a page without applying adhesive directly to the photos. See Chapter 9 for information.

◆ **Speed scrapping.** Refers to the organizational method in preparing for a retreat or class.

◆ **Simple scrapbook.** A nonevent scrapbook dedicated to one specific theme.

Shortcuts

Several different weights of cardstock are available. Go ahead and experiment with them to find what you like, but keep in mind that different weights don't make a practical difference.

Don't Get Stuck—Choosing an Adhesive

I'm going to confess something here that I don't even like to tell my scrapbooking students: I used rubber cement and scotch tape in the first decorative photo album I made for my son! Of course, it was 10 years ago, I was a first-time mother, and I had no clue about scrapbooking other than using clip art and gluing pictures in. Years later, and with much more scrapbook savvy, I know that rubber cement destroys photos, and I now use adhesives that are not only safe for photographs but also affordable and easy to use.

A variety of adhesives exist on the market, and as long as you use one designed for scrapbooking, your photos will be safe. Whether you choose to use glue, tape, or paste is a matter of preference—whatever you find easiest to use and easiest to find. Read on to find out what kinds of adhesives are available.

Singin' the Glues

Glue is available in different styles: There are traditional glue sticks, liquid glue pens, bottled liquid glue, and the current rage is glue dots. Some of these are stronger than others, so try out a few and see what works best for you. Here are some things to keep in mind:

◆ Glue sticks have glue in a stick form. They are a little messy but are reasonably priced and readily available.

◆ If you will be gluing many small objects, a liquid glue pen is a good bet. This type of glue comes in pen form, and glue is distributed depending on the amount of pressure you apply to the tip.

A variety of adhesives are available for safe use in scrapbooks.

◆ Bottled liquid glue distributes glue from a narrow tip that makes it easy to use with small items, such as tiny punches, die cuts, and scraps.

◆ Some glue pens come in a two-way adhesive. This type of glue has a very strong bond when it is wet. If you apply it and let it dry before adhering, the bond becomes temporary, meaning you can remove your photos and embellishments if necessary.

◆ Glue dots are perfect for gluing your three-dimensional accents. They come in a variety of sizes and are very easy to work with.

CK OK Guidelines for Adhesives (for Adhering Paper and Colored Photos to Paper)

Acrylic base or starch base

Reversible

Free from odors, migratory substances, and chemical additives

White or colorless

Nontoxic

Neutral pH: 6.5 to 7.5

After the glue is set, it must not soften, run, transfer, or have odor after it is dry

Must not alter the color of paper, images, or photographs

Must not discolor over time

Must pass the P.A.T. (Photo Activity Test)

More Sticky Stuff

Tape is my favorite adhesive to use in scrapbooks because it's neat and easy to use. A tape roller with its quick-dispensing capabilities and reversible adhesive is a great choice. You can buy refills for it, which also makes it cost-effective.

Double tape has adhesive on both sides. To use it, simply place the tape on your scrapbook page and stick the photo or embellishment to the other side. Double-stick tape is also available in rolls. Just peel it, tear it, and stick it! Nothing could be easier. Tape is great because it doesn't spill and won't dry out like glue. It is also reversible.

From the Archives

The Xyron machine is a popular, though relatively expensive, adhesive option. You run an item through two rollers in the machine, and the machine applies adhesive to one side. Without using heat or electricity, the Xyron can also laminate. You can even create your own stickers with a Xyron! If you plan to do a lot of scrapbooking, consider investing in one.

For precut adhesives, photo splits, sold by the box, are a good option. To use photo splits, simply pull out as many tabs as you need from the dispenser and apply them to your page. Peel off the top layer and apply your photo to the adhesive. That's it!

The "Write" Tools

Be sure to purchase a few writing, or journaling, tools, because journaling is what makes a cute scrapbook into a storybook. At the very least, you need to record the names and dates of the photo subjects, so read on to discover the different options.

A simple, black felt-tip pen is definitely the best for journaling on your pages. The best tool for writing on the backs of photos is a wax or grease pencil, which can be wiped off with a soft cloth, or a special pen called the Pilot Photographic Marker, which is a fine-tip, black permanent pen.

CK OK Guidelines for Ink (in Pens and Markers)

Light-fast/fade-resistant

Waterproof

Odorless when dry, no solvent smell left

High resistance to change, i.e., permanent

Quick-drying

Nonbleeding and nonmigrating quality

Nontoxic

Must pass the P.A.T. (Photo Activity Test) if used with photographs

A Little Protection

Unless you consider fingerprints an embellishment, you'll want to keep your pages in protective sleeves. It is satisfying to finish an extra special page and place it in its protector, and page protectors are great because they're easy to move. You can purchase protectors in a couple forms, from full-page to protectors with sections for photos. These make organizing your photos easy—just slip in the photo, add a note, and you're done. Try giving these protectors to grandparents so they have a place to put all those darling photos you send them.

Shortcuts _____

If you are unsure whether a protector is made with PVC, try the smell test—sniff the product. If it smells like a vinyl shower curtain, don't use it.

Protectors are marketed in two different types: clear or nonglare. The nonglare type has an almost matte-like finish that reduces the glare from the page. I like the look of the clear page protectors, but they do tend to show little nicks and fingerprints more than the nonglare type does. This is, of course, a matter of preference, as both are safe for your books. See which you like best!

Words for Posterity _____

Page protectors are a great way to display and protect your pages. These plastic sheets are available in top- or side-loading styles and come with holes that allow you to place them in a three-ring binder.

Page protectors come in three weights: *economy*, *medium*, and *heavy*. Although all are safe for your photos, there is a cost difference. Economy is the cheapest, and heavy costs the most. Again, this is purely a matter of preference and budget. Although the heavy protectors look nice, they aren't essential to a good scrapbook. Buy what you can afford.

Words for Posterity _____

Economy, medium, and **heavy weight** are terms that refer to the different weights of page protectors available. Economy is lightweight, medium is a bit thicker, and heavy is the thickest.

Do you have a special group of pictures that you don't want to split up? Then try the latest panoramic page protectors—they spread out to show four pages at one time. Try this for your vacation photos that include your oversized photos of the cruise ship you took, along with your tickets and itinerary. These are also great to use with the before and after construction photos you took of your renovated house. Pick up a pack of these the next time you're shopping, and create some great panoramic pages.

CK OK Guidelines for Plastic (for Sheet Protectors, Enclosures, and Encapsulation)

Made of plastic: polypropylene, polyethylene, polyester (Mylar D or Melinex by Dupont)

No polyvinyl chlorides (PVC), commonly known as "vinyl"

Clear, colorless

Odorless

Untreated, no coating on the side next to photograph emulsion or negative

Must not crack or break with age

Must not contain any plasticizers, surface coatings, UV inhibitors, or absorbents and must be guaranteed to be nonyellowing with natural aging

Must pass the P.A.T. (Photo Activity Test)

Cardstock: Backbone for Your Book

Now that you have the photos, some adhesives, and pens to write about your pictures, you need some paper to put everything on. Here's a rundown of basic mounting paper. For detailed information on decorative paper and other ways to use *cardstock* (you know, the cute stuff), see Chapter 5.

Words for Posterity

Cardstock is thick, sturdy paper available in a variety of weights.

The term "mounting paper" refers to cardstock—the usual choice for scrapbooking. Cardstock works well because it is thick and heavy—sturdy enough to mount all sorts of photos and textiles.

Shortcuts

When you use lightweight paper, such as a pattern paper, as a background, it's a good idea to slip a piece of cardstock into the protector so the page will be firmer.

Cardstock is the backbone of scrapbooking. Because it is so sturdy, it holds everything together, and it is very affordable. It costs only 8 to 25 cents a sheet, so you can afford to use this paper for everything—from mounting paper to die cuts to borders.

Typically, cardstock is sold in solid colors, as well as marble and parchment styles. Hundreds of colors are available, so even if you can't find the perfect shade of red to match the photo of the brick on your new house, you'll be able to come pretty close!

CK OK Guidelines for Paper (for Photo Albums, Journals, and Photocopying)

Papers that come in contact with color photographs:

pH of 6.5 to 7.5 and must not exceed 8.0

Alkaline buffered (although unbuffered is recommended)

Lignin-free, 1 percent maximum

Colorfast, no fugitive dye

Must pass the P.A.T. (Photo Activity Test)

Papers that are used with everything else:

pH of 7.0 to 9.5

Buffered with 2 percent minimum calcium carbonate, magnesium, or zinc

Lignin-free, 1 percent maximum

Colorfast, no fugitive dye

This Pen Has a "pH'D"!

I often find great paper at a craft store, but I'm not sure whether it is acid-free. That's when I use a pH testing pen. With a small stroke of the pen, I can tell if the paper is safe to use. It turns a certain color if the paper is acidic, depending on the brand of pen you have. Another use for it is to see if memorabilia, like certificates and cards, are acid-free and safe to put in your book.

The Least You Need to Know

◆ Make sure to find out whether a specific paper is acid-free and safe to use in scrapbooks. Look on the package label, ask the staff, or contact the manufacturer.

◆ Choose adhesives that you find easiest to use and be mindful of reversibility, in case you ever want to unstick something.

◆ Black felt-tip pens are great for writing in your book, and there are special pens and wax pencils to write on the backs and fronts of photographs.

◆ Protect those pages you worked so hard on with page protectors. They'll keep fingerprints off and make sure that what is glued, pasted, or taped stays stuck.

◆ Cardstock is firm, sturdy paper that comes in a variety of colors and weights—use it for all your scrapbook pages.

In This Chapter

- ◆ What you can expect to find inside scrapbooking stores

- ◆ Advice on braving the checkout line

- ◆ What types of classes are available, what you should know before you take one, and what you should bring with you

Scrapbooking Shopping List

1. white cardstock
2. nautical sticker
3. die cuts for birthday/Christmas
4. glue stick
5. protectors
6.
7.
8.
9.

Chapter 4

The Lay of the Land: Scrapbook Stores and Classes

I was overwhelmed the first time I walked into a scrapbook store. I couldn't figure out what all those people were doing buying stationery and fancy paper by the sheet. I thought I was in some sort of deluxe letter-writing place, and I couldn't figure out how to work the die-cut machine. Ladies were lined up with paper in hand, holding these wooden things. I was too proud to ask questions, so I turned around and walked out. I finally got brave and recruited a few friends to take some scrapbooking classes with me.

I've come so far that now I teach scrapbooking classes and workshops. I've learned that many new scrapbookers feel the same sense of confusion I did, so before you run to the scrapbooking store (and run right back out), read this chapter to discover what products you can expect to find and how you can get into a scrapbooking class. After this tour of the scrapbooking store, you will be more confident than I was.

Get to the Source

Where I live in Utah, there are numerous stores dedicated to scrapbooking. In fact, many people from all over the country come to Utah to shop at all the distinct scrapbook stores. Although your community may not have that feature, you will be surprised at how easy it is to ferret out scrapbook supplies.

Following are some ways to find these places:

◆ Many of the major scrapbooking companies, such as Frances Meyer, have a *store locator* on their website that tells you where their products are sold.

> **Words for Posterity**
>
> **Store locator** is a device on websites that requires you to input your zip code or area code and then the data will list nearby stores that sell the company's products.

◆ Look in the backs of some scrapbook magazines for store listings.

◆ Word of mouth—do you have a friend who loves to scrapbook? He or she probably has a favorite place to shop.

◆ Internet message boards—post a query.

◆ You often can contact the manufacturers to find out where to find their products.

◆ Visit www.creatingkeepsakes.com for a store locator.

◆ Oftentimes, scrapbook groups meet at the public library or another city establishment.

◆ A popular feature on some scrapbooking websites, such as the friend finder on www.dmarie.com, will locate someone in your geological area who has registered on their site and give you contact info.

You Better Shop Around

Once you get into a store, you may find that the owners have packed tons of stuff into a very small space. Don't be deceived by a small space; there are still plenty of items for you to look at—and buy. Here are some examples:

◆ **Pens.** Most stores carry a huge variety of pens, all set up in different display racks. Pens are most often organized by brand, not type, so if one company doesn't carry a particular type of pen, check a different one. Be sure to test any pens you like on some scratch paper.

◆ **Die cuts.** Head over to the die-cut section. Make sure to look around for a pricing guide. If you can't see one, ask the clerk for help. Die cuts are sold in many different ways—singly, in packs, or mix and match. You can get more for your money if you buy the die cuts in sets, but there is no need to buy a pack of 10 teddy bears if you will use only 1 or 2. Just be sure to avoid surprises by figuring out the pricing system before you head to the cash register.

◆ **Stickers.** Take a look at these. It's likely that there is a price guide nearby. Some of the stickers, like Mrs. Grossman's, have letters on the back that correspond to a pricing key. Some stickers are sold singly, others are sold by the sheet, but most stores insist that once you cut a sticker from the rack, you have to buy it.

◆ **Paper.** If you go to the scrapbook store to pick up a particular pattern or other kind of paper, only to find out that the store no longer carries it, let the clerk know. Often, staff can tell you if they have any more on order or if they've discontinued that pattern. A salesperson may even let you know of other stores in the area that carry that pattern.

◆ **Storage.** In this section, you will find all sorts of fabulous items made specifically to stash your scrapbook supplies. These items range from binders made to contain your stickers and accents to luggagelike totes made to contain everything you need to scrapbook on the go.

◆ **Albums/protectors.** It's amazing how many different types of albums are available; your only hope is that you can make up your mind. You will see different types of albums—we will discuss this later (see Chapter 8)—and you will also see a section of protectors in a broad range of different sizes and finishes.

◆ **Accents.** If you are looking for decorative accents, templates, or stickers that focus on a specific theme, such as bowling or hiking, the clerks in the shop can be very helpful. They know the store's inventory, often have a good idea whether they have anything that matches what you need, and can direct you to the product.

◆ **New items.** One of the most fun things to do when you walk into a scrapbook store is to go straight to the display of new items. This is where you can find the latest scrapbooking tools and products. Seeing these can give you the motivation and inspiration to try something new.

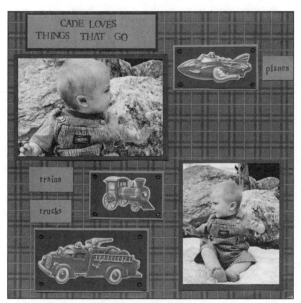

This layout was inspired by the display at the front of a scrapbook store showing the new products just arrived.

Divide and Conquer

If the store is divided into sections by items, you will probably find all of the cardstock together, which is helpful. Two choices are usually available for cardstock—by the sheet or in packs. I recommend buying cardstock by the sheet, except for the colors you know you are going to use often, such as white or black. It is commonly less expensive to purchase cardstock in a pack, but there is always a color in there that you won't use—guaranteed. I still have bright orange and hot pink from a pack I bought (I've used it up by letting my kids make paper airplanes out of it). Purchasing the paper by the sheet is my recommendation.

Shortcuts

If possible, organize your purchases by product—stickers, die cuts, pens, and so on. This speeds up your checkout process because the cashier won't have to keep pulling out different price charts.

You will typically find pattern paper and stationery organized by color, size, or theme. If you need to purchase some pink pattern paper, for example, go right over to the pink section and find what you need. If you need birthday paper, then do the same. The price is often found on the back or on the wall above the paper.

Now that you're loaded down with paper, pens, stickers, and more, it's time to head to the checkout. This can be scary, but remember, you are making an investment in your family.

Shortcuts _____

Some scrapbooking stores offer free basics classes to beginning scrapbookers—find out if your store does and take advantage of it!

Not only will the checkout be where you can buy all your supplies, it is often where you'll find information about upcoming events and places to sign up for scrapbooking workshops and classes. Most stores offer calendars with activities and workshops, so be sure to pick one up. If they have a mailing list, put your name on it; you'll be the first to know about any sales and specials.

The Internet Is Your Friend— Shopping Online

Shopping online is great for those who don't live close to a scrapbooking store or don't have time to visit one in person. From the comfort of your own home, you can browse through all sorts of scrapbooking products. Some of these websites feature "shopping carts," which makes it easy to order directly from their sites with a credit card. Or if you prefer, you can print up an order form, fill it out, and fax or mail it to them.

There are many different online stores. Some feature only one product, such as stickers or pens, while others sell one line of products. You'll discover many hard-to-find items online, so even if you do live close to a scrapbooking store, check out the virtual stores just to see what's out there.

While it is sometimes difficult to tell exactly what you are getting when you see it on your computer screen, most stores offer a product guarantee—if you aren't satisfied with what you purchase, they will give you a refund or exchange.

Here are some of my favorite online general scrapbooking shopping sites:

- **www.twopeasinabucket.com.** All-inclusive site, message board, layout gallery, and ideas updated monthly.
- **www.gonescrappin.com.** Fabulous country feel with great layouts listing the products used.
- **www.pebblesinmypocket.com.** One of the first in "cute" providers of scrapbook products.
- **www.memorymavens.com.** Friendly staff, great selection of what is new, a real communitylike feel.
- **www.scrappinfools.com.** Whimsical-looking and abundant selection of mixed media.
- **www.DMarie.com.** Very reliable and consistent.
- **www.scrapbooks.com.** Great prices and a perfect place to start.
- **www.crafterstoybox.com.** Extensive selection of punches.
- **www.lsslinks.com.** This site will find local stores in your area for you.
- **www.foxtales.net.** Great selection of pint-size albums with instructions for completing them.
- **www.catSCRAPPIN.com.** For the cat lover.
- **www.croppingcorner.com.** Offers a 30-day money-back guarantee, and prices are usually cheaper than the suggested retail price.
- **www.scrapbookersparadise.com.** For Canadians.

These are just a few of the online store services. For more, see Appendix A. I suggest looking at some scrapbooking magazines for color photos of some of these products so you can check them out before you buy.

Here are a few online shopping tips:

◆ Order with a friend to save on shipping.

◆ Check the sites often for good deals.

◆ Utilize their message and chat boards to find some scrapbooking connections.

◆ If you are always looking for new products, most of these sites list their new items under a special heading.

◆ Most online stores have a free newsletter that will inform you of new products and upcoming specials.

◆ When you can, shop at nonpeak hours to cut down on the waiting time.

◆ Search through the links to find helpful new sites.

◆ Empower yourself as a consumer and send comments and suggestions about what you want—this industry responds well to the consumer.

Shopping at Your Local Hobby and Craft Store

Even if you are not close to a store that specializes in scrapbooking supplies, your local craft or sewing store will often have some products. Even Wal-Mart carries some products in their craft section, so everyone should be able to find something. The great thing about these stores is their prices! Although they might have a limited inventory, they are reasonably priced.

Sticky Points

Unfortunately, people who go to the large stores to purchase scrapbook items sometimes find that stock is limited and the aisles are constantly a mess. Try talking with the store buyer to see when they get new shipments so you can get first choice.

When you are at a hobby or fabric store, head over to the craft section and see what products they carry. You can usually find lots of prepackaged kits. There might be a birthday kit, for example, that includes stickers, paper, and die cuts, as well as suggestions and instructions. Other popular kits include baby, wedding, vacation, and pet themes. These stores usually carry the basic scrapbooking accessories like scissors, adhesives, and trimmers. Sometimes, stores can special order things for you, too—just ask. And many craft stores are beginning to offer scrapbooking classes.

Shortcuts

Make it a point to speak to the store manager about scrapbooking items and ask whether they are planning to carry more. This input lets managers know there is a need and may convince them to increase their scrapbooking supplies inventory.

Shop Smart—Save Time

When shopping for a shirt to match your new blazer, you bring the blazer to the store with you, right? Of course! You can't tell what will match unless you have the item with you. The same holds true for scrapbooking. If you are shopping for a particular shade of orange or red to match the sunset in your photo, by all means, bring the photo with you.

Efficiency Counts

Many people waste time and money at the scrapbooking store when they shop without a purpose. They wander leisurely through the aisles looking for the perfect item to pop out at them. If you have time and money to spare, this is probably fine. But if you want to be a little more efficient, two methods work for me.

If you live near a scrapbook store and can make frequent trips for items as needed, bring the pictures you are working on to the store. That way, you can decide at the shop what items you want for a particular layout. I also make a list of basics that I need as I am scrapbooking. When I run out of photo splits, for example, I jot it down so that I know to pick them up on my next trip.

If you don't want to make frequent trips, buy in bulk. Make a list of what you need and want before you go to the store and stock up. There are a few items you'll always need—pens, page protectors, and adhesives—so go ahead and buy plenty of these. As for accents and other items, jot down what you need according to category. For example, for baby pages, you'll need stickers, die cuts, pastel paper; for pet pages, you'll need paw print stamps, bone die cuts, and sticker letters. Do this for as many pictures as you think you'll have time to complete before your next shopping trip. Bring a friend with you to make sure you don't go overboard and make sure you have fun!

Scrapbooking Shopping List

1. white cardstock
2. nautical sticker
3. die cuts for birthday/Christmas
4. glue stick
5. protectors
6.
7.
8.
9.

Make a list, check it twice.

"Stick" to a Budget When Buying Stickers

Many people complain about how much money they spend on scrapbooking. When I ask them what it is they are purchasing, they usually give one of two answers.

Some people buy every tool available, including punches, puzzle mates, scissors, pens, and shape cutters, and then they purchase paper and other perishable items. When I ask them why they get all those tools, they say they just have to have everything. So I say, well, either budget yourself or don't complain. If you are someone who likes to have all of the latest tools, which can add up, give yourself a budget that you feel good about and stick to it. You will appreciate the tools you do buy even more.

Other people buy paper and stickers, take them home, and never use them, so of course it seems to them that they are spending an outrageous amount and they aren't getting anything out of their purchases. If this is you, try to buy what you know you are going to use, even if this means going to the store once a week and spending only $5.

Remember not to overbuy, because you will get frustrated and laden down with too many products and choices. Purchase items you know you will use. Shopping sales, clipping coupons, and shopping around are some ways you are guaranteed to get more for your money. Good luck!

Workshops, Crops, Snips, and Snaps

I have taught scrapbook classes for the past three years in numerous stores, and I have also attended many classes. Scrapbook instructors typically are avid scrapbookers and enjoy the hobby so much they can easily inspire others. You can learn a lot from your instructor; so if you take a class, be sure to ask plenty of questions.

There are two types of scrapbook classes:

◆ **Specialty classes.** In these you work on a specific technique, such as making paper dolls. The instructor leads the class as she or he talks about a certain technique. Some of these classes include a project that participants complete that night with the help of the instructor, and, in some of them, the instructors teach something ongoing, such as photography or page design. You are sure to come out of these classes with great examples and idea pages.

From the Archives

Scrapbooking classes are so much the rage at consumer trade shows that it is almost impossible to get a spot if you haven't signed up early. The instructors at these classes are the creators of scrapbook products, representatives for different scrapbook companies, and professional scrapbookers. You can expect all sorts of goodies at these classes and tips from the professionals.

◆ **Workshops, crops, snips, and scraps.** At these classes, a scrapbook store generally provides nonperishable supplies such as scissors, punches, and templates for you to use during the class. You'll also have an instructor who can help you with ideas for using the products you've bought and who can give suggestions to help finish those impossible pages.

Shortcuts

Ask friends who often attend classes who their favorite instructor is. You will be sure to have success if you go to a great instructor.

Don't have a store in your area that offers scrapbooking classes? If you already know a group of people who like to scrap, decide what you as a group are most interested in learning. Select group members to research and prepare a short instructional class for others in the group when you meet again. This can be a great way to learn in a less formal setting. You will definitely feel comfortable asking questions, and you will learn when it is your turn to present something to the group. If you get a large enough group together, you may be able to get experts to come to you. This is a great, inexpensive way to learn.

Picking and Choosing—Deciding Which Class to Take

I enjoy learning new techniques but get bored easily, so the class I take had better be hopping or I won't recommend it. When deciding on a class, look for something that appeals to you. Don't waste your time taking a class on punch art if you don't own or like punches.

I have often had people take my basics class who have already been scrapbooking for a year and are just looking for ideas. They are disappointed when I discuss the bare bones of scrapbooking—something they are already familiar with. When signing up for a class, ask the clerks what the class is about and what you will learn. Get the details before you sign up so you won't be wasting your time.

Shortcuts

Envious of your friend in a neighboring town who takes all sorts of fun classes at her local scrapbook store that yours doesn't offer? Go to the store manager or owner and tell them the classes you are interested in taking. Chances are they will even offer the class you are looking for.

See what the store has to offer, and be selective. Don't be afraid to attend by yourself—you can often glean more from the class if you aren't chatting with your friends. If you are just beginning to scrap, start with a basics class and then attend a workshop. If you are looking for some inspiration, try a design class. If you find that you are suffering from scrapper's block, try attending a class where you make accents that you can use on your pages, such as 3-D layouts or a journaling class. The idea is for you to leave inspired to try something new in your scrapbook and feeling as if you have completed something.

Sharpen Your Pencils—Preparing for Class

A few tips on preparing for class:

1. So you don't attend the class unprepared and end up being frustrated, find out what you should bring with you when you sign up. Do you need to bring glue, scissors, pictures? Always bring your favorite pen and some paper to take notes on. You can accomplish so much more if you prepare your pictures before attending a workshop and select the photographs you are going to work on.

Sticky Points

Remember to be a little discreet at workshops, especially because the photographs and writing you are including tend to be very personal. (One participant in a class I heard about was having a good time looking at everyone's pictures and commenting on them until she looked at someone's album and saw her ex-husband with the album owner's friend! Oops!)

2. Categorize the pictures you want to complete before the class so you can use class time more effectively. If you are working on your child's birthday pictures, divide the pictures into pages. For example, children playing party games, kids eating cake, party guests, opening presents, and so forth.

3. Get an idea of the accents you want to use—for a birthday page, do you want to use birthday accents, such as balloons, or do you want to stick with the dinosaur theme your child chose? Bring what you will be using to the class.

4. Bring only the necessary supplies to class. You don't need to bring your tackle box full of punches since you can usually use the store's punches. You will need your adhesives, both cardstock and decorative paper, and pens. The store does provide cutting tools, and, of course, you can purchase anything you need. (I like to bring my favorite cutters and straight-edge scissors with me so I don't have to share.)

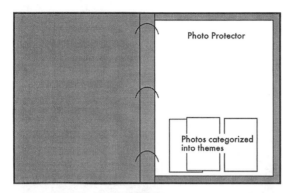

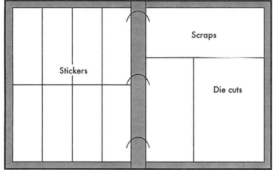

Your binder with stickers, scraps and die cuts.

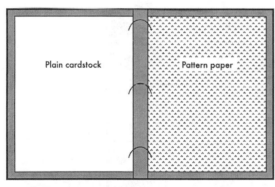

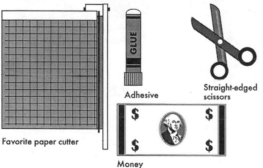

With these supplies and a good class, you'll be ready to scrap the night away.

5. When you are at the class, take advantage of having all of the materials on hand to select accents and colors that go well with your pictures. I like to gather all of the supplies needed to complete my page, such as paper, die cuts, and stickers, and put them in a protector to finish at home. That way I am taking advantage of being in the store. I can always glue and journal at home, but I don't have 500 pieces of paper to select from.

The Least You Need to Know

- To find a store near you, go online to a store locator or post a message.

- Bring your photos along when you shop to avoid wasted purchases.

- Whatever stage of scrapbooking you are in, beginner or more advanced, try taking a class to learn new techniques and meet fellow scrappers.

- If there are no classes where you live, try starting one. Gather a group of scrappers together and find out what people would like to learn. Have everyone pitch in to create lessons for the others.

- Prepare for classes by finding out what you'll need and organizing photos and supplies beforehand.

In This Part

Part 2

Setting Up Shop

You'll be truly amazed when you discover all the products and services available to the scrapbooker. Every time my husband accompanies me to the scrapbook store he's utterly shocked to see the variety of paper, pens, and stickers available. In this part, you'll read about the wide variety of products available to the scrapbooker and what you can do with them. Refer to this part often for ideas on using these products.

In This Chapter

◆ Decorative papers and patterns—it's like having an artist draw in your book!

◆ Use patterned paper to tie together the theme of your scrapbook.

◆ Pattern paper and specialty paper can be used for all sorts of craft projects.

◆ Think texture—try using velvety, wavy, metallic, or handmade papers.

Chapter 5

All Paper Is Not Created Equal

My sister came with me on one of my visits to the scrapbook store. "Oh my gosh!" she said, "I love all this paper, but why do you need so many different kinds? I'm intimidated by all the choices!" I remember feeling the same way when I started scrapbooking. Not only are there different types of paper—cardstock, stationery, paper packs, and patterned paper—but each category has many variations. Between color choices, sizes, weights, and patterns, typical scrapbook stores stock anywhere from 500 to 2,000 different types of decorative paper! That's why I've dedicated an entire chapter to this subject.

Scrapbooking paper can be used for more than scrapbooking. I've used it to make party invitations and greeting cards, and my friend Marcia sent me a lovely baby announcement made with scrapbooking materials. It's a good idea to be familiar with the different types of decorative paper, and after reading this chapter, you'll realize that quality paper is worth the few extra pennies.

When I was a cashier at a scrapbooking store, I loved seeing women come in with their boyfriends or spouses. I remember one particular incident, when a pregnant woman came in with her husband. He stood, bored, in the corner of the store as she oohed and aahed over the adorable baby-patterned paper. After half an hour, he cleared his throat, and his wife got the hint. She trundled up with a shopping basket overflowing with paper. He stayed motionless in his corner until I began ringing up her purchases. Suddenly he came to life, "Hey!" he said, "I think your machine is broken. There is no way that piece of paper costs 50 cents."

That's when I explained to him what I'm about to explain to you: All paper is not created equal.

Are You Beginning to Notice a Pattern?

Although the rooms in my house are painted a neutral white like many homes in the United States, I love patterns. My twins' bedroom sports nautical wallpaper, and my bedroom is decorated with a floral wallpaper border. Patterns are terrific because they give dimension and warmth to a room. From dots to checks to stripes, patterns are exciting. One of the best things about a scrapbook is that you can experiment with as many different patterns as you like without committing to painting a wall in your house with lime green and hot pink stripes. And since there are so many patterns to choose from, each page can be fresh and exciting.

Pattern paper is by far the most popular scrapbooking paper. Everyone incorporates it into his or her books in some way or another. There are two types of pattern papers—specific and general.

This baby layout uses paper that is made just for babies.

Words for Posterity

Pattern paper is paper with designs repeated on the entire page. Designs range from bold to conservative, funky to tasteful. Pattern paper is a fun addition for your scrapbook.

From the "Specific" ...

Specific pattern paper is paper designed to enhance pages that focus on a specific theme, such as weddings, graduations, or birthdays.

Shortcuts

Specific pattern paper lets you use somebody else's artwork to enhance your pages. Many companies, such as Frances Meyer, offer coordinating stickers to match their pattern paper. With products like these, you can't go wrong! It's the next best thing to hiring a professional to draw in your scrapbook for you.

These types of pages can boost your scrapbooking power. For example, when my second son, Justin, was born, my husband was in school. Because money was tight, I didn't take many baby photos of him (something I still regret). To make up for it, when I did his baby book, I bought a lot of specific paper, like the baby's first step paper. Although I didn't have an actual picture of his first steps, I managed to find a photo of him when he was about the right age and make a cute page out of it. This way I could still document his milestones and accomplishments. (Of course, now I take tons of photos, so many that my kids ask me to please put the camera away!)

The pattern paper on this layout is perfect for the title.

One word of caution: Specific pattern paper is fabulous, but if a whole scrapbook is filled with it, your personality may be muffled a bit. To minimize this, some of the companies that offer specific pattern paper also offer coordinating general pattern paper. So while your pages will match, they won't get the reaction, "Look at how cute these pages are, never mind the photos!" Another solution is to use some of the specific paper to mount your photos on and cut letters for your title out of the rest.

Try to use just part of the specific pattern paper so as not to overwhelm your layout.

From the Archives

It's best to buy specific pattern paper only when you've got a definite use for it, although scrapbookers have been known to stage photos in order to use a paper they absolutely love.

... to the "General"

The other kind of pattern paper is called "general pattern paper." This type of paper incorporates patterns, such as dots, florals, and stripes. This paper works great on any of your pages and can be used in all sorts of combinations. Try to echo the mood of the photo with the color and pattern of the paper you choose.

Using the general pattern paper as a background sheet lends excitement and movement to the photos.

Try using just a portion of the paper as your background.

General pattern paper is so versatile that one design can be used many different ways. Take the mini red dots for example: With this one kind of pattern, you can create pages for the Fourth of July, Valentine's Day, or Christmas. You can use it to record your college or high school days, make an "I Love You Because …" page, or highlight an anniversary dinner. These are just a few ways to use one pattern. With all of the styles available, you can create an infinite amount of pages!

Shortcuts

General pattern paper is made to be used for any occasion. Go ahead and stock up on it—you can use it in hundreds of different combinations.

Here you see the colors of the pattern paper reflecting the mood of the photos.

Uses for Pattern Paper

The following are a few of my favorite uses for pattern paper.

◆ Individual photo mounts—Mounting a snapshot on pattern paper makes it pop out from the page. You can combine two coordinating papers for even more fun.

This is one of my favorite ways to use pattern paper.

◆ Die-cut layering—Die cuts are shapes made out of paper. You don't have to stick to solid colors to make them. The key to using patterns for die cuts is to choose small-scale patterns; large-scale patterns won't show up well.

◆ If you're like me, you hate to throw out small scraps of pretty pattern paper but don't know what to do with it. Try using a punching tool to make little *punches* that

will match your page. Punches are small tools used to punch little shapes out of paper. If you have more scraps left, place several colors randomly on a page to create a patchwork look.

A perfect use for your scrap bin.

◆ Paper piecing is a lot of fun. Paper piecing is the process of creating a layered look with templates by tracing and cutting different pieces of paper and combining all together for a layered look. While you need some solids for this technique, a few small areas with pattern paper will look great.

◆ Using pattern paper for your letters adds a special touch to your page.

◆ You can mount items other than photos on pattern paper—titles, captions, and journaling look great used this way.

The flower pattern reflects
the pictures perfectly.

The pattern paper works
well here as an accent.

Words for Posterity

Punches are small tools used to punch designs out of paper. The designs are also called punches. (See Chapter 9 for more on die cuts, punches, and other embellishments that make your pages look great.)

You can use pattern paper to carry out the theme of your layout. Do this by selecting specific pattern paper for the background and a solid-colored cardstock to mount your photos on. Add embellishments and some journaling for a beautiful page.

Many new scrapbookers are wary of using photographs they have had taken at professional studios in their albums. But properly preserved in a scrapbook, these pictures will last longer than if you put them in a frame or leave them in those cardboard mattes they give you. Besides, professional portraits look wonderful in albums. The trick is to choose a pattern paper that matches the theme of the portrait without overshadowing the photograph.

I like to take the pattern paper, both specific and general, and use it in *colorblocking* layouts. This is a great technique that doesn't overwhelm but still adds a flavor of fun.

It is also fun to take some of your scraps of pattern paper and use it as bits and pieces on your layouts—economical, too.

You will be able to find a use for all of that fabulous pattern paper now available.

Words for Posterity

Colorblocking is a design technique in which you place "blocks" of paper on your background block style.

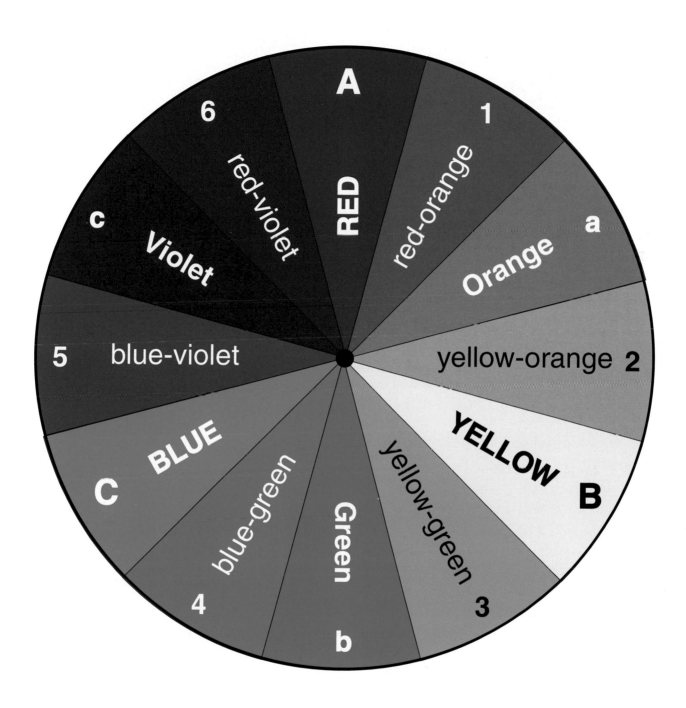

China Cove
beach

Many summer
vacations were spent
here as a child. It was fun
to go back with my
family. I always loved the
blue and green of the
water. It was nice to see
it hadn't changed.

...enjoying the view...

The colors used in this layout, created by Robin Johnson, reinforce the emotion behind the photo.

A Festival of Fall Colors

Joselyn had a fun fieldtrip to the Day's Farm. All the joy school kids got to ride on a tractor to the pumpkin patch! She got to pick out her very own pumpkin.

You can use vellum in many different ways to accent your photos. This layout by Robin Johnson is a lovely example.

You can complete pages fast using pre-illustrated products such as those featured in this "Boys Will Be Boys" layout by Beary Patch.

Mixed media adds flair to this "Pals" layout.

SISTERS

Sisters are two different flowers from the same garden

When using pre-illustrated products, don't get carried away with "sticker splatter." Here, the use of the floral sticker, by Treehouse Design, is perfect.

Here you see another simple use of stickers in this layout with my niece Chloe.

in yourself

others

Dare to

Breanne

believe

inspire

dream

I love this photo of my niece Breanne, and I didn't want to overwhelm the layout with accents. The wire words by Making Memories fit in nicely.

On The Fly

Three-fourths of the Earth's surface is water, and one-fourth is land. It is quite clear that the good Lord intended us to spend triple the amount of time fishing as taking care of the lawn.

~ Chuck Clark

The only thing I can say about this layout is I promised my husband, Kent, I would include a page of him doing his favorite thing—fishing!

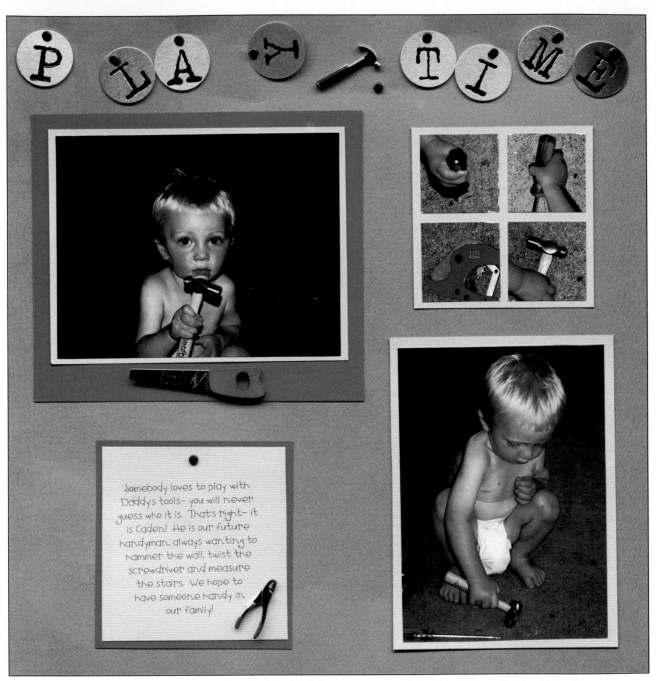

Somebody loves to play with Daddy's tools- you will never guess who it is. That's right- it is Caden! He is our future handyman, always wanting to hammer the wall, twist the screwdriver and measure the stairs. We hope to have someone handy in our family!

Metal accents add crispness and a look of intrigue to this layout.

These shaker boxes were fun to create and add movement to this captured memory.

EMMIE

you go girl!

Mixed-media meets stickers—to create a fabulous accessory for your
pages, these stickers by Card Connection accent the layout just right.

In
Your
Eyes

check out those lashes-
long eyelashes is a
Smedley family trait!
one physical trait that
every one of our sons
has is long eyelashes.
Here we see a side view
of Caden and Nathan.
I can get lost in their
eyes, I can stare at my
children for hours. I
am amazed that I
had a hand in bringing
them to the earth.

To capture emotion, use familiar sayings, quotes, or expressions, such as the one used here.

lazy
days

After winter comes the summer.

After night comes the dawn.

And after every storm,

there comes clear, open skies.

Samuel Rutherford, Scottish Author

brad
chloe
emmie

These bright tags are a favorite of mine. Use them for titles, journaling, or just as they are.

I love using unique letters, and these Scrabble look-a-likes are fun on this page.

A California Fall

Taylor and I
traveled from
the snowy mountains
to the warm fall in
California we loved it.

Using preserved elements from nature gives this layout a unique look.

Try dividing the layout in half
as I did on this one.

Here it is used on the bottom
half and framed.

Take your pattern paper and
put some down the side.

Two overlapping strips work great with
this layout.

In this double-page layout, the use of the pattern paper is repeated using the same technique on the other side.

Placing a strip down the center works well.

Stationery—Not Just for Writing Letters

Stationery is marvelous for easy pages, especially when your pictures match the theme of the paper. Select your pictures and try to find stationery that coordinates with the theme and color of the pictures. Put pictures directly on the stationery or mount your photos on a coordinating cardstock color. What satisfaction!

A fun project you can do with stationery to jazz up your books is to create divider pages. Here's how you do it:

1. Decide how you want to divide your books. If you are doing a scrapbook about your trip to Europe, you can divide the book according to country. If you are doing a chronological year, you can divide according to season.

I love you up to the moon
And I love you as big as the sky
I love to watch you sleep
I love to hold you when you cry...
One day, when you are older
And taller than me
I'll say I watched you grow
Like a beautiful tree...
I love you up to the moon
And I love you as big as the sky
You'll always be my little man
Love you the best that a mama can
...And one day if you rise up
And call me blessed
I'll say it was a joy
To give you my best...
'Cause I love you up to the moon
I love you as big as the sky
I love you up to the moon
I love you to the moon

Here we see stationery with
a poem in the middle.

Words for Posterity

Stationery is paper with a decorative border that is blank on the inside. It makes great notepaper and wonderful scrapbook pages.

2. Choose stationery that goes with your theme. When I did dividers by the seasons in a year, I chose stationery with a border of snowmen for winter, gardening tools for spring, seashells for summer, and autumn leaves for fall.

Sticky Points

When creating divider pages, use the same company's paper to avoid a cluttered look.

So. Davis Soccer 1999

Center your portrait picture for a perfectly easy page.

Shortcuts

When mounting photos on decorative paper, cut out the inside of the paper that won't show to use in another project. This saves money!

3. Decide what you want to put on the stationery pages. I like to journal about what we do that time of year, important events, family outings—anything that gives a general idea about our history. A photograph depicting that season would work, too. Compile your pages and include them in your scrapbook. I think you will find this adds a great touch to your book.

Another favorite way to use these full sheets is to cut the designs out and use them as enhancements on your page. You don't need to include the entire design; instead, you can use elements from the stationery and adhere them to your page. Once, I was looking for frogs to put on a page I did of my little boys wading in water looking for frogs. Stickers weren't the right size and the die cuts I had were too large. I found some stationery with frogs on it and cut them out. Perfect!

When using smaller stationery, try pulling elements out of the stationery to embellish your page. For example, if you're using stationery with an illustration of the cow jumping over the moon with a photo of your baby sleeping, pull out the main elements of the card, such as the cow and the moon and stars. You can re-create those designs using punches, die cuts, or stickers. Make sure you stick with the same color scheme, though.

I like to look at stationery for ideas on how to lay out my own pages. The way they overlap the designs can be truly inspired. Use these as a guide to creating your own pages.

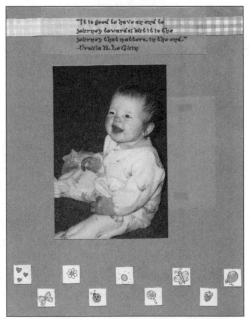

The accents on this page came from a stationery page that I cut up.

Stationery paper is for more than scrapbooking! Look at all the fun things you can do with it:

◆ Try this instead of sending a stuffy, formal thank-you card: Take a photo of the recipient using the gift. Adhere this to the middle of a piece of stationery that matches the gift. (If you received a book, for example, use stationery with a studious theme.) Write a message beneath the photo, sign, and send!

◆ Stationery pages make great starting points for scrapbook pages about trips—write the dates of the trip and where you went inside the border … and away you go.

◆ If you're tired of spending tons of money on holiday gift cards, take a different approach. Mount a photo in the middle of some cheery holiday paper and write a simple note. Add a sticker or two, and you've got a card that's sure to be appreciated!

Shortcuts

When making these cards, carry out the design of the card in your pages. For example, if the stationery border has a wavy edge, perhaps you could cut your photos with decorative scissors to mimic it.

◆ Stationery comes in a variety of animal themes—a perfect way to announce the addition of a new pet to your family!

Take out the Guesswork— Specialty Paper Books

For those of you who have a hard time selecting pattern paper, several companies have a solution. They offer specialty paper books that come in specific and general pattern paper. There are layout examples with instructions that show the reader what to do. Some of them also have coordinating stickers and templates to use with these pages. I'll bet you don't leave these books sitting around—they are very user-friendly.

The best thing about these books is that they take the guesswork out of matching your pattern papers. Just choose a theme, and you'll find a book with all sorts of coordinating florals. If plaids are what you need, you'll be sure to find a book with plaids in it, too. Some of the books have matching punch-outs. Sold separately, the punch-outs are a more economical option than stickers, and they match the paper packs.

From the Archives

This shows how scrapbooking has taken off—Hot Off the Press Paper Company introduced its first 15 Paper Pizzazz specialty paper books in 1997. They now sell 185 different books! According to them, their most popular theme books include Disney, wedding, and baby books.

This layout was a breeze—all the paper and accents match perfectly and are contained in one book.

Don't forget to think of your kids' own scrapbooking projects when looking at these books. You can supply the scissors and glue; all the kids need is the paper in the books and the coordinating punch-outs. Their books will look great because the paper and punch-outs match.

The combination of papers on this layout is all that is needed.

This paper is already colorblocked. Use it for a quick and easy layout.

Shiny, Soft, Speckled, or Wavy—More Specialty Paper

I am in awe at the variety of paper now available. From vellum to vivelle, you are certain to find something that will suit your every wish.

Corrugated paper is heavy, wavy cardstock. It is a great way to add detail to your layouts. I like to use it in scenery layouts—as leaves or blades of grass, for example. Used sparingly, corrugated paper attracts the eye to a specific photo. Next time you go to make letter die cuts, think about using this paper instead of the flat stuff for words that pop out.

Don't forget the bright, shiny, glossy, and metallic papers—a favorite of teenagers. These certainly attract attention. Take it from me, you won't be able to take your eye off some of these. It's great to use these papers, but remember, a little goes a long way. Use silver to make a mirror or use the glossy paper in your school colors for an original look.

There is also a growing selection of *pre-embossed papers*—cardstock with a raised design. You can color over the designs to add detail or leave them plain for a simple, elegant look.

Another way to add texture to your scrapbook is using handmade paper. This paper often has flowers, grasses, or other natural-looking items pressed in it. It is a favorite choice for a unique and simple look.

This layout combines shiny pre-embossed paper for an out-of-this-world look.

Want to add a little elegance to your pages? Try vellum. This strong, translucent paper is currently available in a variety of solid colors and patterns, including speckled. I love to use it for journaling on a special page or to put as a frame around a photo. This paper is quite versatile. There is an idea book called *Designing with Vellum,* by Robin

Johnson, published by Autumn Leaves, that shows all of the different ways to use vellum. (See color insert for layouts from the book.)

The handmade paper adds to the natural look of the layout.

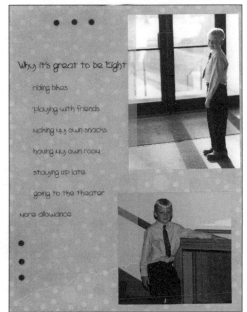

Here is one of the most popular uses for vellum—journaling.

Vellum can also be used as a unique embellishment. One of my students used it as steam rising off a bowl of soup. You can also use it as smoke from a chimney, clouds in the sky, or try some pink vellum as cotton candy! And vellum isn't just for scrapbooks—it also makes lovely baby announcements and wedding or bridal shower invitations. Try layering the colors over each other for a unique look.

The overlayed vellum adds a variety of colors.

The Least You Need to Know

◆ Finding the right paper is key to the look of your book. You can find paper to match almost any theme or color you can imagine.

◆ Decorative paper comes in specific (themes like holidays, weddings) and general (stripes, checks, dots, florals, and plaids) patterns.

◆ Pattern paper and stationery can be used to make holiday cards and baby announcements—be daring and experiment!

◆ Specialty papers, such as velveteen, vellum, handmade paper, or corrugated cardstock, can help make your layouts real knockouts.

In This Chapter

◆ Add life to your scrapbooks with writing

◆ What makes a pen safe (and durable) for a scrapbook

◆ Plain to fancy—pens, pencils, and other tools for drawing and enhancing scrapbook pages

◆ Lettering techniques for everyone

Chapter 6

Doodle On!

A scrapbook is more than pictures stuck on pages. It is a story, and although the photos are often the focus of the story, you need words to tell the reader who and what are in the pictures. (See Chapter 12 for more information on creating compelling text for your scrapbooks.) When writing in a scrapbook, you must have the proper tools, tools that will let your ancestors read your writing in 100 years. Pens ought to have ink that is safe and lasting.

There are numerous types of archival-quality pens in all sorts of colors, styles, and price ranges, so you'll find one to suit all your needs. The scrapbook store where I teach workshops has an entire aisle of pens!

If you've got neat, attractive handwriting, you're set. If you are like most people, you might be able to use a little help in the penmanship department so that your journaling will not only be legible, but charming, too.

This chapter describes the amazing range of pens available and what you can expect each type to do. I will also give you information on where to go for lettering techniques books, websites, and so on.

Permanently Safe

A pen is safe to use in your scrapbook if it is any or all of the following:

◆ Permanent   ◆ Quick-drying   ◆ Nonbleeding
◆ Waterproof   ◆ Pigment ink   ◆ Nontoxic
◆ Fade-resistant

Sticky Points

Make sure that the ink in the pens you use is CK OK approved if they will be used with photographs.

Most of the pens found at a scrapbook store have all these qualities, but look carefully at pen labels at your craft and other art supply stores because not all pens are suitable for scrapbooking. Many more options exist than just black, felt-tip pens, although it is the simplest and usually most legible option for recording history. Felt-tip pens come in a wide variety of tips, point sizes, and colors that can make a big difference in the look of the writing in your book.

Fine-tip point pens, for example, range in point size from .005mm to .08mm and are good for journaling and lettering. Fine-tip pens offer the widest range of small tip sizes and can be found at scrapbook stores, general craft stores, art supply stores, and stationery stores.

(Layout by Stephanie Bryson)

This title was created with a fine-tip black marker.

Words for Posterity

Fine-tip point pens are pens with extremely small tips and are good for doodling and precise lettering.

Fancy It Up a Little

There are a number of elegant and interesting choices when it comes to pen tips that will give your pages loads of style.

Calligraphy Pens

Calligraphy pens can create grand-looking titles and captions. The trick is in the tip of the pen, which is what is used to create formal lettering. They are available in different sizes and colors. The tips on these pens are flat and broad, so when they are held at a 45-degree angle, they produce letters that are beautiful and ribbonlike. Even if you've never taken a calligraphy class, you can still do some simple strokes with these pens that will add a lot of elegance to your page.

Sticky Points

Be gentle with your fine-tip pens—they're not designed to stay firm under pressure. When writing with them, press only as hard as you need to and use a thicker pen to color in broader areas.

From the Archives

Calligraphy comes from the Greek words meaning "beautiful writing." Before books were printed with movable type on printing presses, documents were painstakingly drawn by calligraphy artists. Beautifully leather-bound, illuminated calligraphic manuscripts can be found in fine art museums. Fine writing was so prized in the fifteenth century that a line of script by a Persian calligraphy artist named Mir Imad was sold for a gold piece!

(Layout by Nikki Maw)

I enjoy the more fancy hand-lettering on this layout.

From the Archives

The most popular scrapbooking pen system is the Zig Memory System, made by EK Success. It has a comprehensive selection of markers: calligraphy, brush, fine, bullet, and scroll tips, each of which comes in 24 colors. They also have opaque markers, so pretty much anything you need, Zig sells.

Paint It on with Paint Pens

With many different tip sizes and over a dozen different colors, opaque paint pens boost your creativity. You can find them at scrapbook stores. Paint pens show up on dark cardstock where felt-tip pens can't. The gold and white paint pens are my favorites because they lend a royal look to my pages.

(Layout by Nikki Maw)

This layout using a small-tip paint pen works well on dark paper.

If you like the look of paint pens, you'll want to try gel-based rollers. They come in a variety of tip sizes and colors, from basic black and green to outrageous fluorescent pink and purple. Be sure to try the milky colors on your dark pages. Don't overlook the lightning variety—colors mixed with silver—for a futuristic look. These pens are great for journaling and are goof-proof!

Fine and chisel pens feature two ends—one small felt tip and one with a slanted tip. A must-have for the creative letterer, use it to create lettering in all sizes.

The tips of paint pens are often soft, like brushes, and you control the amount of ink that comes out by the pressure that is applied to the tip.

Colored Pencils

Colored pencils are an exciting new addition to the repertoire of scrapbooking writing instruments. Zig and Berol Prisma make sets that are photo-safe and affordable. They come in kits of assorted colors. Many art-supply companies make colored pencils, too, but they are not guaranteed to be safe to use in scrapbooks, so be sure to check. Colored pencils can come in sets of 12, 24, 48, or 64 or more colors. Use them to doodle, write titles or captions, or color on your pages. Another great feature of using colored pencils is that you can use them to shade your pictures, something that is hard to do with pens.

Chalking

A fairly new technique used in scrapbooking to add color and dimension to your scrapbooking is with chalks. You can buy these in pencil form or tablet form. The pencils are much easier to use. Try chalking on your die cuts and paper for a dimensional look.

(Layout by Stephanie Bryson)

Gel pens are used in this layout for journaling.

Shortcuts _____

Bring along some scratch paper to the store so you can "test drive" a pen before buying it. All the pens have different feels, and you'll want one that is comfortable to use and gives you the line you want. Buy extras of your favorite colors when they are on sale.

(Layout by Stephanie Bryson)

Title touched up with chalk.

It's Not All Black and White

If you ever sort through old pictures of your family, you'll notice that many black-and-white photographs from the 1920s or 1930s, especially those that look like they were taken at a professional studio, are colored—and this is long before color film was available. Those pictures were taken with black and white film and had color added after they were developed. This is sometimes done today with old black-and-white movies and is called "colorizing." Some people don't like the way colorized films look, figuring that black and white was the way they were meant to be viewed, but you can make some very neat effects by adding color to black-and-white pictures.

Shortcuts

If the paint pens are too messy for you, try the milky gel roller pens on dark paper. You may find that when you are using these, you can concentrate on what you're writing instead of how you're writing it.

If you would like to add color to your black-and-white photos, tools are available that will let you do it at home. Previously, only oils were available for this purpose, and they required a high degree of expertise—and a large investment (for more information on these, see Appendix A). But now you can get black-and-white, hand-coloring pens in a set that usually includes coloring pens in basic colors, pre-moistening solution, a dye-remover pen, a sponge, and some cotton pads. The dye remover pen makes the process foolproof; if you mess up, all you need to do is correct your mistake with the dye-remover pen and try again.

Lettering Techniques for the "Il'letter'ate"

When I am teaching workshops, this question inevitably comes up in the class, "Who has neat handwriting?" Most everyone answers, "Not me!" You may not feel confident now, but with some practice, you can create pretty, handwritten titles for your pages. By taking a class or practicing our alphabet on the next page, you'll be able to whip up some great titles. Here are some basic steps to start yourself down the path to becoming a creative letterer.

Shortcuts

Colored pencils are a classic revision tool for the scrapbooker. They come in a variety of colors and are great for coloring in your borders, titles, or anything.

First, find some lettering styles that you like and want to duplicate. You may like the look of block lettering best, so focus on supplies and techniques that will help you draw block letters. If you like all types of lettering, pick a starting point. One lettering expert I talked to advises starting with a basic alphabet and practicing this alphabet to create a strong foundation for lettering that you can build on. Here are some of her suggestions:

1. Keep the spacing between the letters, words, and lines even; use a ruler to pencil in some lines if you need to.

2. Keep the size of the letters the same; pencil in lines at the top and bottom to give you an idea of your boundaries.

3. It is important to have an even slope throughout the letters. Keep your vertical lines parallel.

Keep these three basic suggestions in mind as you begin duplicating the alphabet. It's best to pencil in your letters first. This gives you a preview of how the lettering will turn out. Experiment with different pen tips to create different looks.

Shortcuts _____

A basic alphabet is the beginning point for other lettering creations.

Keep on practicing the starter alphabet until you feel confident, then add to it. The ways are only limited by your imagination. Here are some sure-fire ways to get you going:

◆ Try different pen widths; the fat widths are bolder and attract more attention. The thinner tips are more delicate and soft. You can manipulate the lettering look simply with your choice of pen width.

◆ Add a simple *serif* style—such as dots, hearts, or squares—to the letters at the end point of each stroke.

Words for Posterity _____

In lettering, a **serif** is the decorative line that extends from a letter, or its "foot." The typeface used in this sidebar is "sans serif," or without any decorative serifs.

◆ Layer the letters. You can do this by outlining in another color and then coloring it in, or you can outline part of the letters and leave spots to fill in with doodles or colors that match your page.

◆ Stretching your alphabet higher or lower will give you a different look.

◆ Mix upper- and lowercase letters of the same alphabet to create a distinct look.

◆ You don't always have to keep your lettering in a straight line. Try curving it or tilting the letters for a playful look.

◆ Experiment with different pen tips—try chisel, calligraphy, or even an opaque marker to see what you can create.

Shortcuts _____

If you can't get the lettering down, you can always trace it onto your pages with a tracing table or tracing paper.

When incorporating creative lettering into your pages, remember that you don't want to use too many different styles of lettering on the same page. Pick a style that will support the theme of your pages. For example, don't use a formal script style for camping photos; save that for more formal events, such as weddings or graduations.

(Layout by Nikki Marx)

Title with spice.

Get the Red Out

Okay, imagine this: You take a great group photo where, miraculously, everyone is smiling and has their eyes open. It would be a perfect picture except for all those red eyes. We have all had this happen from the flash! A red-eye pen is the solution to this problem. Dab a bit of this ink on the red spots and, although it doesn't restore the true eye color, it does take the red away. If this is a frequent problem for you, it's definitely worth the investment. These pens are available in scrapbook stores and in camera equipment and supply stores. There are also ones available for pets.

Shortcuts

Use a red-eye pen to dab out annoying "red eye" from your photos.

The Least You Need to Know

◆ Writing and drawing tools should be permanent, fade-resistant, waterproof, and quick-drying.

◆ The right pen makes all the difference in the look of your writing, so be sure to try several different kinds first.

◆ Pens are available in different colors and types for different effects, including calligraphy pens, paint pens, gel-based pens, and more.

◆ Use colored pencils and pens for drawing and decorating.

◆ Anyone can learn to become a better letterer. First, try mastering a basic alphabet, and then experiment with pens and different techniques. You can also take a lettering class.

In This Chapter

◆ Not just scissors—different tools for cutting a straight edge

◆ How to get the most out of decorative scissors

◆ Cutting perfect shapes with special tools such as shape makers, personal die-cut machines, and punches

◆ Why templates can be a scrapper's best friend

◆ Incorporating layout design using templates

Chapter 7

Snip, Snip! Multi-Use Cutting Tools and Templates

Around the world, people are clicking their cameras an average of 46 million times a day. That's a lot of photos! Although many of these photos go straight into an album as is, many others are trimmed, cropped, or cut. And while some people grab the kitchen shears to do the cutting, dozens of tools can be found that are better suited for the job.

This chapter updates you on the different straight-edge cutting tools and gives you the scoop on those funky decorative scissors. I will tell you all about templates, what they are, how they are useful to scrapbookers, and all the different kinds available, from letter to puzzle types. If you are a big fan of cutting your pictures into shapes, you are going to love tools called shape cutters, which effortlessly cut photos into all kinds of interesting and perfect shapes. For those who love using shapes, personal die-cut machines are available from a few different companies.

Hey, Cut It Out!

Many scrappers like to embellish their pages with complimentary shapes that reinforce the layout—read on to find how best to do this using tools that are created to cut that perfect shape. When I first started scrapbooking in 1996, decorative scissors were all the rage. That fad has faded but these tools can still be used to add whimsy to your pages.

Straight-Edge Scissors

I like to have a large range of cutting tools at my fingertips when I work on my scrapbooks. Scissors are the most basic cutting tools for trimming and cutting everything from photographs to textiles to other documents you might incorporate into a scrapbook. You must have a pair of large scissors to scrapbook. While many people use their sewing scissors for this, I suggest purchasing paper scissors because they are designed for the job. Large scissors (with eight-inch blades) work well and are needed for cutting big shapes and templates. You'll also need some small, sharp scissors to cut detailed shapes from stationery and trim around tight corners. My favorite new tool is the small scissors from Fiskars with a non-stick coating. I also recommend a *paper trimmer* or paper cutter for absolutely straight edges.

> **Words for Posterity**
>
> **Paper trimmers** are terrific tools that are easy to use. Simply place your paper in the trimmer, line it up on the grid where you want to make a cut, and move the blade down.

If you don't like scissors, you can try a rotary paper edger. While it was originally designed for quilters, scrapbookers have fallen in love with this tool. The paper edger has ten interchangeable blades and is easier on your hands than scissors. It'll take a little practice to become proficient, so try it out on some scratch paper first.

Trimmers and Cutters

For straight-edge cutting, you can use anything from a lightweight small cutter to a large office-type cutter. There are two basic types of cutters: the type with an arm handle that you pull down to cut the paper and the kind that has a sliding blade. I suggest that when considering the purchase of a large paper cutter, you shop around and try some out. The difference between the two is minimal, and choosing one is a matter of preference. Trimmers with sliding blades seem to give more control over the cutting than arm handle trimmers and typically you can purchase replacement blades.

The straight edges on this layout were quick and easy with my favorite paper trimmer.

Scallops and Ripples—Using Decorative Scissors

"What are these for?" is a familiar refrain I hear from people who see decorative scissors for the first time. *Decorative scissors* are a fun way to add a touch of whimsy to your pages. Because the scissors come in so many patterns, you can find one to match any mood and theme!

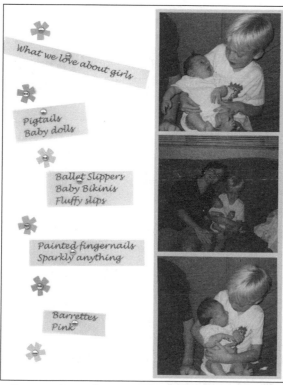

What we love about girls

Pigtails
Baby dolls

Ballet Slippers
Baby Bikinis
Fluffy slips

Painted fingernails
Sparkly anything

Barrettes
Pink

Decorative edges work well on this layout.

Here are the five most popular decorative scissors patterns and uses for each:

◆ **Victorian.** These scissors have an elegant look with curves and waves that hearken back to the Victorian era. Use these scissors when doing wedding, heritage, or classic portraits.

◆ **Majestic.** This is a bold pattern that can also be used to create an elegant page. I like to use these when I am doing pages that need attention drawn to the pictures. Try using these scissors with your favorite family portrait pages or to create stately borders for your heritage pages.

◆ **Scallop.** You can use these playful scissors for just about anything. It can look like miniature bubbles for your tubby-time photos, or you can use it with baby pictures to resemble the edge of a blanket. My favorite way to use it is to cut paper with it and then punch holes in the curve to look like lace.

◆ **Pinking.** Try using it with your camping pages to reinforce majestic mountains in the background. I also like to use it when I am using a sun to highlight the sun's rays shining down.

◆ **Ripple.** These are versatile scissors with a series of small curves in a variety of sizes. Use these to duplicate sand or water or to add depth to your pages.

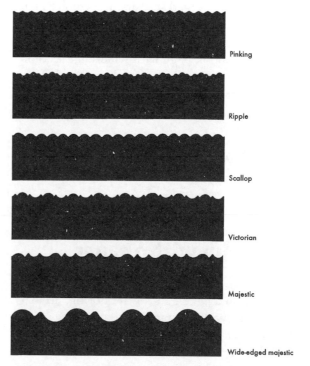

Pinking

Ripple

Scallop

Victorian

Majestic

Wide-edged majestic

Here are patterns produced by Victorian, Majestic, Scallop, Pinking, and Ripple decorative scissors.

Corner-edger scissors are designed to add flair to the corners of your pages, photos, or mounts. I like to cut the corner of the background paper with these scissors and cut out a photo mount with the same pattern. This gives my page consistency.

Words for Posterity

Corner-edger scissors cut just corners. Each pair creates four different types of corners.

A fun new addition to decorative scissors is *wide-edge scissors* that make a cut up to five times as deep as regular decorative scissors. While you may not reach for this tool as often as your deckle-edged scissors, it is good to have a few of your favorite designs on hand. To create a stunning look, try cutting the sides of an entire scrapbook page with wide-edge scissors and placing a coordinating color of cardstock behind that to keep it flowing.

Words for Posterity

Wide-edge scissors are decorative-edge scissors whose cut is five times deeper than normal scissors.

Mix It Up with Shapes

Sometimes, seeing the same sized 4×6 photos lined up on a page gets a little boring, no matter how cleverly you angle the pictures. Cutting pictures into shapes can add interest and flair to a scrapbook, but it can be frustrating to cut circles and ovals with scissors, even with a template to trace. Fortunately, shape cutters take care of this problem. These are available in every shape imaginable. You can buy separate blades and templates such as the

Coluzzle and cut in graduating sizes. Also available for the scrapbooker are swivel blades that cut inside a shape template. My only suggestion is to try them before you buy. Different brands have different feels, and you want the one that works best for you.

The shapes in this layout were cut with a swivel blade and a template—quick and mistake-proof.

From the Archives

The first decorative tool used for scrapbooking can be traced back to the decorative scissors such as Fiskars. Scrapbookers loved using these to cut strips of paper, photo mats, and background paper.

One of the best times to cut your pictures into shapes is when you have gotten back a roll of film with parts that were overexposed or if the pictures turned out badly altogether but you still need to put them in. (Or try it if you want to cut out a relative or ex-significant others who are no longer "in the picture"!)

Shortcuts

When using decorative or plain scissors, move the paper rather than the scissors for a more accurate, straight line.

Often people ask: When should I cut my photos into shapes? It's really a matter of personal preference and depends on what you're trying to achieve with that particular layout. I find that I rarely cut my photos into shapes because it is too time-consuming, but I think that when you want to emphasize a photo or add movement to the layout this is a good way to do so.

JUNIOR JAZZ BASKETBALL 2002

See how the photo cut into a circle draws in attention.

Tempting Templates

Templates have been on the scrapbooking scene from the beginning. Originally, templates were available in only a few basic shapes, but now you can find themed templates, too, such as medical, automotive, animal, and other unique choices, as well as letter templates, paper doll templates, and puzzle designs.

Chloe is All Dressed Up and ready to go

"I love to wear pretty colors and lots of jingley jewelery," says Chloe.

This layout using a PuzzleMates template is charming.

Words for Posterity

Templates are plastic sheets with shapes and designs cut out so you can trace the shapes and use them. Basic templates have shapes such as ovals and circles.

If you don't have access to a shape cutter, use the basic templates to cut out squares, circles, ovals, and other shapes. To get the best results, trace over your photo with a grease pencil, cut, and wipe off the excess. If you get tired of seeing the same old rectangular photos on your pages, shape templates will quickly add interest to your pages.

A great addition to the template scene is the Plan-a-Page template. These templates overlay your page and show where your photos and journaling should go. To get a different look all you have to do is turn them sideways or upside down. Great for page design.

The design on this layout was a breeze using the Plan-a-Page template.

Letters to Trace

Letter templates are great! I love bright headings for my pages, so I use them frequently. I like to cut letters out of vibrant pattern paper. While this can be a little time-consuming, it produces a wonderful, crisp look. You can trace and color the letters, trace and cut the letters out, trace and decorate the letters using stamps or

sponged ink, or trace and cut the letters out of more than one color of paper. The possibilities are endless.

Letter templates come in a variety of sizes. The small ones are extremely time-consuming to cut out, so I like to use those when I trace and color. The medium and large ones are great to trace and cut or trace and color. Try overlapping the letters to create fun titles. When you have to do a poster for the PTA fund-raiser, don't forget about your large letter templates. They definitely attract attention. Watch out, or you may be appointed the publicity chairperson!

Words for Posterity

Letter templates are templates with the alphabet. Use them to create great page headings.

Shortcuts

For clean-cut marks, turn your template over and trace on the back of your paper. This way you will achieve clean-cut lines.

Specialty Templates

Specialty templates have designs cut out that match a theme. A medical template might have items such as a stethoscope, bandages, crutches, and a doctor bag. Take the stethoscope and use it for a layout on your baby's first trip to the doctor. (And be sure to include the growth charts you receive.)

The best specialty templates are often the ones you can't find other accents for, such as Noah's Ark.

Create page headings with letter templates.

Remember, you don't have to use templates just to cut designs out. You can use them as stencils to trace a design directly on your paper and then fill it in with permanent pens or other writing utensils. Add some details for a personal touch. For example, if you have a template of animal designs and you are making a page about the birthday party your children threw for their pets or a trip to the zoo, you could trace the outline of a cat, dog, or elephant and add whiskers, eyes, ears, details of fur, and even a tusk with a colored pencil or pen.

If you'd like a more artistic look, place the template on the page, and, using a rubber stamp pad, sponge some ink in the design; you don't have to trace an outline because the sponged ink will be in the shape of the design.

A Place to Write

Journaling templates are a must-have for all who like to write on their pages but can't keep their lines straight. My favorite is one called Journaling Genie, made by Chatterbox Publications. These templates provide you with writing guides for small, medium, and large lettering. You can even find lettering guides in different shapes. To use, simply trace the lines on your pages with a light pencil, write your captions, and erase the pencil.

Words for Posterity

Journaling templates are templates made to create unique lettering. You can letter in different shapes or lines.

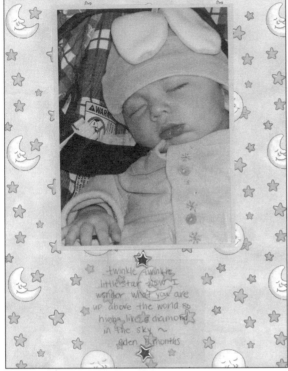

Journaling Genie layout.

As a fun project, buy a small spiral-bound scrapbook and let your children trace in their favorite Journaling Genie shapes. Then they can write memories about their trips, stories, or whatever else they want. Placing pictures that go with the described events would be great fun. Use this scrapbook to emphasize the journaling. This helps encourage your child to have fun while writing and recording memories.

Sticky Points

Puzzle templates are a great way to use up all those extra birthday pictures to create a great page, but don't use pictures that are one-of-a-kind because they all get blended in with these layouts.

(Layout by Julie Rasmussen)

Star PuzzleMates layout with template.

Words for Posterity

Puzzle templates are simple tools that allow you to create puzzles out of your pictures—a fun look that can jazz up a layout.

The Perfect Shape Every Time

You don't have the patience for cutting out the designs yourself; you want something a little more, say, perfect. Try using shapes made from die-cutting machines. Many scrapbook stores have their own and allow you to use them. These machines are simple to master and require little effort to operate. Ask for a demonstration at your local scrapbook store and you will be on your die-cutting way. If you don't have access to a die-cut machine you can purchase pre-cut dies individually or in packs. They are great to use as accents and can be easily personalized.

These die-cut accents were purchased in a theme pack.

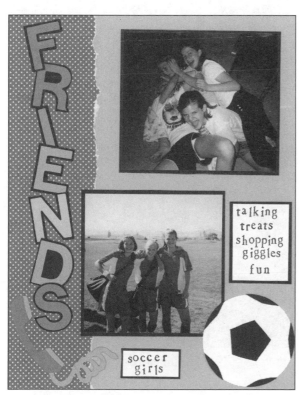

Here is a layout using some single dies I purchased.

One of the latest trends in scrapbooking is laser die-cuts. These are fun to use and add a dimension that traditional die cuts can't.

Punch It Out

It is amazing the collection of products we scrapbookers accumulate and I have to say I am among them. Collecting punches is a passion with some and I can see why. These hand-held shape cutters are fabulous to have on hand for a number of projects. The variety of shapes and sizes available is mind-boggling. There are classes dedicated to punch art and groups that exchange punchies (paper punched into different shapes) on a monthly basis.

Basic punch shapes enhance this layout.

Punches don't come only in basic shapes. Try using a border punch—this punch is long and skinny and meant to be used as a border. You can also get punches that are made to punch only corners. These can add a decorative look to your page, photo, or mat corners. Don't forget to use the silhouette punches. These punch out exactly what you think they won't—that is, they punch out the outline around the shape instead of the shape itself. Try doing this on one color of cardstock and mounting a coordinating color beneath it for a unique accent.

**This subtle border punch
is a perfect accent.**

To add dimension, use pattern paper with your punches and try to layer them by cutting the same shape out in different colors and then cutting these and layering them for a more realistic look.

Layered punches—sailboat.

The Least You Need to Know

◆ You can use decorative-edge scissors to create jazzy edges on your photos and paper. Try a Victorian edge or a Majestic look.

◆ Trimmers cut your photos into great shapes, such as ovals, circles, or squares.

◆ Templates come in a huge variety of shapes and designs, from letters of the alphabet, to fun shapes like animals and boats you can trace, to journaling templates with space for writing.

◆ For a unique page, try a puzzle template and have your child put the pieces back together.

In This Chapter

- ◆ Choosing an album
- ◆ Matching the look of an album to the theme of your scrapbook
- ◆ Options to personalize your album cover
- ◆ Easy project—covering an album with a fun fabric

Chapter 8

Cover the Basics: Choosing the Right Scrapbook Album

Choosing an *album* to house your scrapbook pages is important. You want the album to look good, of course, and you might also want it to match the theme of a particular scrapbook. A friend recently showed me a photo album of a trip to Greece—because the book focused on travel, she had decorated the cover with a map of the world, and it looked great. You also want an album to suit your needs for size and storage capabilities, and to be very easy to flip through (which, hopefully, you'll be doing a lot).

As for which album sizes and features are best, this chapter contains information on available sizes and features and the best ways to make your album look special on the outside as well as the inside.

The Ties That Bind

A primary difference among albums is the way the pages are bound into place. Some albums use a simple and effective *three-ring binder*, while others hold their pages with attractive and interesting posts or *straps*. The other major difference among albums is the paper size used.

Words for Posterity

An **album** is a blank book or binder used to store photographs and scrapbook pages.

Words for Posterity

Three-ring binders look like loose-leaf notebooks and have three metal rings of varying sizes to attach the album covers and hold pages. They are affordable and enable you to rearrange pages easily. Books with **strap** bindings have plastic straps that run through a holder directly on the pages and keep the book in place.

When trying to decide which type °of album to use, consider the following:

1. What kind of album is most accessible to you?
2. Do you foresee the need to move your pages around?
3. Where will you store your albums?
4. How many pictures do you want to use in each album?
5. Do you plan to use computer clip art directly on your pages?
6. Do you foresee color copying your pages for use in future books?
7. What is your budget?

8. Do you live close to a scrapbooking store?
9. Do you plan to maintain the same size for all of your future binders?

Shortcuts

When you are looking at three-ring binders, be sure to get a kind of binder ring called a "D ring"—this type of metal ring has a flat side that allows pictures to lay flat when the binder is closed.

Once you make your choice and start, you may find that it is challenging to switch over to another type. I decided once that because I had always used the $8\frac{1}{2} \times 11$ album size, I would use a 12×12 album for my children's baby books. I love the look of the large pages, and I just wanted to try it out. I went out and bought everything to make three baby books—even all the extra inserts and page protectors. The problem was that whenever I sat down to put a page down, I found that I couldn't create pleasing layouts. I was so used to using the other size that I found it frustrating to do larger pages. Eventually, I sold my blank 12×12 albums to a friend. I have talked with scrapbookers who successfully go back and forth between the two sizes. Mainly, they use the $8\frac{1}{2} \times 11$-inch binders, and they use the larger-sized albums for theme books such as Christmas and vacation.

Aside from size, when looking for an album you should think about what elements are important to you. Some people like large pages but want them to be easier to move around. A solution for this is to get three-ring binders and protectors that hold big pages.

Three-Ring Binders

Three-ring binders are easy to use and very versatile. They come in a variety of pre-made covers, from padded vinyl to tapestry, are inexpensive, and the pages can be moved around without a hassle. The downside is that when you open the binder, the left-hand page is not flush with the right-hand page, but separated by the rings.

Three-ring binder with corresponding title page.

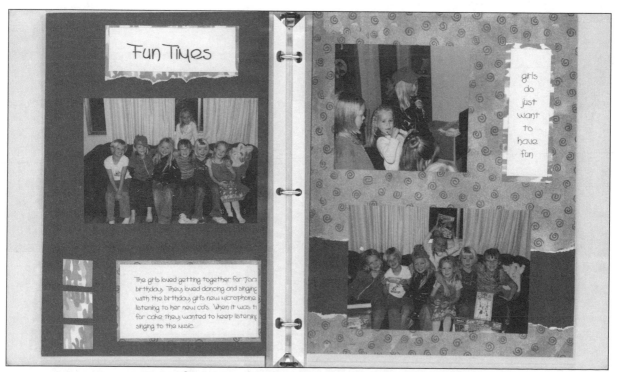

Open three-ring binder showing pages side by side.

Plastic Strap Bindings

Albums that have a plastic strap binding can be expanded. One of the nicest things about these albums is that, unlike three-ring binders, which have gaps in between the pages, these pages lie flat, with no gap, so your layout is continuous from the left-hand page to the right-hand page. The only drawback with these albums is that it can be challenging to move pages around since you put pictures on both the front and back of pages. If you ever need to take the pages out for a school poster or something, it is more complicated because you have to take all of the pages out to get to the one that you need.

From the Archives

The most popular type of album among all scrapbookers is the plastic strap binding album by Creative Memories, one of the pioneers in the industry.

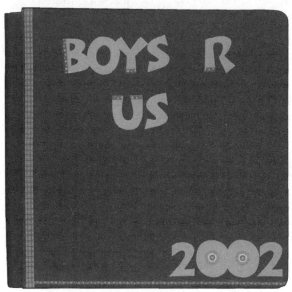

Basic plastic strap binding album with decorated cover.

Open plastic strap binding album with pages flush.

Post-Bound Albums

Another choice is *post-bound albums,* which have a metal post that holds pages tightly bound together like a book. Many post-bound albums have printed designs on the album covers and are expandable by moving the pages. To fasten extra pages into these kinds of albums, you have to punch holes directly into scrapbook pages. This album is probably not the best choice if you are going to have little children flipping through it because the pages can easily tear.

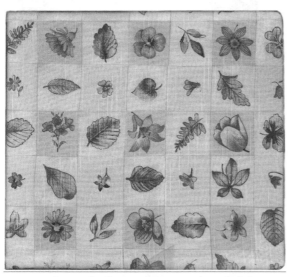

Post-bound album decorated with fabric (see the "Fabulous Fabrics" section later in this chapter).

Words for Posterity

A **post-bound album** is held together with a metal post that runs through the pages.

Open post-bound album.

Spiral Binding

Spiral-bound books come in a variety of sizes with pages that can't be moved around. These books are a great choice for children's scrapbooks. The pages won't get lost, and for kids, the smaller sizes are perfect. These books can be purchased with writing and embellishments already on the pages. All you need to do is add your pictures, and you're done.

Words for Posterity

Spiral-bound books have a metal or plastic spiral binding.

Spiral-bound album with decorated cover.

Open spiral-bound album.

Sticky Points

Still can't decide which scrapbook to choose? Talk to your friends and neighbors and see what they suggest. If you don't know anyone who scrapbooks, try going online and posting questions. You will be sure to hear opinions from many scrapbookers on what album sizes and types they use and why.

Why Size Matters

Albums for scrapbooks come in two main sizes: 8½ × 11 and 12 × 12. Not sure which size album to use? Circle the answer that is closest to your scrapbooking style:

1. My goal in scrapbooking is …

   a. To get as many pictures on a page as possible.

   b. To make cute pages.

2. When it comes to scrapbooking, I am more concerned about …

   a. Keeping down the cost of supplies and equipment.

   b. The way my pages look.

3. An ideal scrapbook page is …

   a. Lots of pictures and lots of journaling.

   b. Pictures and some scrapbooking.

4. When shopping for scrapbooking supplies …

   a. I will look high and low for desired products.

   b. I want to be able to find everything I need without a lot of searching.

5. I want my scrapbook to …

   a. Look different from the rest.

   b. Be the same as everyone else's.

See which letter you choose more of. More "a" choices, and you might want the 12 × 12 album. More "b" choices, and you may prefer the 8½ × 11 album.

Each has its own advantages and disadvantages. Advantages to using the 8½ × 11 books:

◆ There is a much larger selection of decorative paper.

◆ Paper for these books is usually less expensive.

◆ Books are readily available.

◆ Books are smaller and easier to transport.

◆ Smaller pages may be easier for some people to work on.

◆ It's easy to switch pages around.

Disadvantages of using 8½ × 11 albums:

◆ They don't hold as many pictures on a page.

◆ Pages don't lie flush so layouts aren't continuous.

◆ It's easy to spend a lot of money on paper because there is a larger selection.

◆ There is less room for large portraits such as 8 × 10s.

Following are the advantages of using a 12 × 12-size album:

◆ This size allows you to fit more pictures on each page.

◆ Layouts lie flush so the look is more continuous.

◆ Albums encourage you to be organized because you use the front and back of each page.

◆ Albums have a classic look because of their size.

Following are disadvantages of using the larger books:

◆ The albums and pages are typically more expensive.

◆ Pages aren't simple to move around.

◆ There is a smaller selection of decorative paper.

Shortcuts

There are companies that make templates specifically for decorating album covers, so check your local craft store to see what is available.

One of the most practical issues when choosing an album size, of course, is the number of pictures that you want to put inside. When using the 12 × 12, if you average 6 pictures on a page, you can get about 45 pages front and back in an album. Therefore, you can put as many as 540 pictures in that album! If you have that many photographs to put into a book, the bigger size is your best bet.

Using an 8½ × 11 three-ring binder, you'll average 4 pictures on a page. With 40 pages front and back in a binder, you can put approximately 320 pictures in an album. Either way, you can fit a large number of pictures into albums of these sizes.

There are multiple small album choices out there with different types of bindings. These smaller albums are great for all sorts of projects, like making simple albums for your children, Grandma's *brag book*, any gift album, and for times when you just want to do something simple and fast.

Words for Posterity

A **brag book** is an album especially for parents, grandparents, and other proud relatives. Anyone who will whip out pictures of their kids and grandkids at the drop of a hat will appreciate one of these. Use a small album they can carry around with them and fill it with pictures of the little ones. Leave some blank pages in the back and, every so often, send them updated photos.

Here is one of my favorite small albums.

You *Can* Judge an Album by Its Cover

The cover of your album is the first thing people will see when they look through it. Like the cover of a book, an album cover can convey the mood and theme of the scrapbook inside. A cover can be a simple, classy leather with gold lettering—this says serious elegance. Or it can be a personalized cover with all kinds of artistic and decorative embellishments. Either kind functions to heighten a viewer's anticipation of what will be inside.

Of course, you can purchase your albums with already-made, nice-looking covers, or you can try to dress your covers up a bit. Here are some suggestions on how to decorate and personalize album covers.

You can even personalize pre-made albums such as this one.

Decorating Blank Album Covers

Some albums come with blank canvas covers that are great to personalize. There are many wonderful decorative options. For example, you can use stamps or templates on the cover—stamp or trace on designs and leave them outlined or color them in. If you are an artist, you can draw on covers to your heart's content. Because covers will be most exposed to the elements, don't forget that you always want to use permanent waterproof markers for cover art.

My son loves to use spiral-bound albums and decorates the covers using stickers. I have seen some albums made with wood covers—think of all the possibilities you have with a cover like this: rubber stamps, rub-ons, iron-on fabric, and wood stains. This is another great thing to use to decorate your covers.

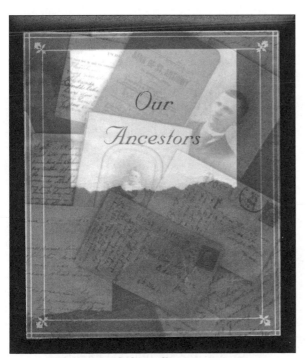

I decorated this album using my scrapbooking materials.

Fabulous Fabrics

Another nice decorative idea is to use fabric to cover an album; most stores carry already-made versions in tapestry, denim, and other types. Or try to make your own fabric-covered album. This is a great way to tie your cover together with the theme of the album.

If you want to do this, look at your photos to decide what you want to use to cover the album. For general scrapbooks, pick a favorite fabric that suits all needs, such as plaids or stripes. For books that have more specific pages or themes, get a suitable fabric. A travel book, for example, could be covered with a stamp tapestry, showing stamps from all over the world.

Fabric Possibilities

Here are some interesting possible covering fabrics:

- **Plaid dish towels.** I have heard of people using nice-quality plaid oversized dish-towels to cover their albums.
- **Animal print fabric/fake fur.** If you are an animal lover or just a member of the wild kingdom, try this one.
- **Formal fabric.** Try satin for a wedding, velvet for formals, taffeta for proms.
- **Denim.** You could use fabric or old jeans for a great cover.
- **Flannel.** Soft, cuddly, and rustic.
- **Holiday fabric.** For those pictures of your favorite holidays.
- **Sports prints.** For that album full of sports pictures, newspaper clippings, and ribbons.

This rich nautical binder is made of tapestry.

Sticky Points

The adhesive on contact paper isn't safe, so try to avoid using it for album covers. Instead, use the Xyron machine (see Chapter 3) to laminate and apply safe adhesive at the same time.

Fabric Cover Project

After you have chosen a fabric you like, follow these directions on how you can use it to cover an album front and back. These easy steps will work on a three-ring binder or with a post- or strap-bound album that will allow you to disassemble the album while you cover it.

Supplies you'll need:

◆ Depending on the size of your book, enough fabric to cut out fabric two inches wider than the album

◆ The album you intend to cover

◆ Tape

◆ Glue

◆ Scissors

◆ Decorative paper or cardstock for inside front and back covers

Follow these steps:

1. Lay fabric out on a flat surface, printed side down, so that the pattern goes on the outside of the book. Open album and lay it out flat in the middle of the fabric. Cut fabric all the way around the album about two inches wider than the album.

2. When fabric is cut, begin folding fabric on the inside front cover. Snip the corners of the material and fold the fabric over each inside front corner. Tape the corner fabric down. Then fold down the fabric along the top and bottom sides. If you have to, make a small cut in the fabric so that it will fold down near the spine. Just tuck the fabric in under the metal that holds the ring binder. Tape down the fabric along all the sides.

3. When the inside front cover is done, fold the fabric along the back inside cover the same way, starting with cutting the corners, covering the book corners with fabric, and then folding the material over the inside back cover.

4. When both front and back covers are taped, try opening and closing the album. If it feels like the fabric is pulling too tightly when you try to close the album, loosen the fabric along the back inside cover and retape.

5. When there is enough slack in the fabric, permanently glue the folded fabric around both inside and back covers. After you have glued the fabric down, trim your two pieces of decorative paper or cardstock to a size about a half-inch smaller than your covers and glue them into the inside back and front covers. (This covers up the ends of the fabric and gives your book a finished look.)

Cover tips:

1. Try finding a material that conveys your album's theme. Fabric and notion stores usually have a great selection ranging from kid's patterns to fancy satin and lace. And because you are buying a small amount, you don't have to worry too much about the cost.

2. Once you've covered the book, if it seems like there is too much extra fabric folded inside the covers, trim it down.

3. Use some of your fabric scraps inside your album for continuity.

Creative Collages

Or try this cover idea: Assemble a *collage* of items that correspond with the theme of your book or that you just think look interesting together, make a color copy of it, and use it on the cover. Here are some ideas:

◆ If your book is about your daughter's graduation from high school, put together a collage of photos of her from grade school to graduation, make a color copy of the collage, and make that part of the cover.

◆ For a book about a particular year in your family's life or in your life, gather newspaper and magazine clippings, pictures, and headlines of noteworthy news items from that year, make a collage out of them, make copies of the collage, and make this the cover.

◆ Use postcards from your Alaskan cruise to make a cover for your travel album.

◆ Try using a map charting your route on the cover so you can look at where you traveled in comparison to where you live.

◆ For performers and musicians, paste your favorite piece of music or your playbills on the cover.

> **Words for Posterity**
>
> A **collage** is an artistic composition made of various materials (such as paper, cloth, or wood) and glued onto a surface.

Store Your Albums, but Not Too Well

The whole idea of having your photos displayed in an album is to contain the pages and protect them so you can view and enjoy your pictures any time you want. The best type of storage for your albums is a high-quality, acid-free album with a slipcase to keep dust, dirt, fingerprints, and light away from your photos. Store albums upright on a bookshelf where dust and dirt are unlikely to settle onto the pages.

Remember to store albums where temperatures don't fluctuate dramatically and they aren't exposed to bright light. Of course, you always want them easily accessible so you can look at them, but the kinder you treat them, the longer they will last.

The Least You Need to Know

◆ Three-ring binders are convenient—you can rearrange your pages anytime you like.

◆ How many pictures do you have to present? Pick an album size that all your pictures fit into.

◆ Try personalizing album covers with fabric, stickers, paintings, and drawings. Tie a cover to the theme of your book and make it fun!

◆ Store your albums to keep pictures safe but make sure you can get to them easily. You want to enjoy looking at the albums you work so hard to make.

In This Chapter

◆ Adding pizzazz to any page

◆ Framing your photos with pre-illustrated frames

◆ Making your titles look professional with page toppers and frame-ups

◆ Personalize your paper dolls

Chapter 9

Pre-Illustrated Goodies and Gadgets That Give Your Scrapbook Flair

Here is where the fun begins! Now that you know the basics of scrapbooking, from the essential tools to scrapbookese to making sure that the products you use are safe for photographs, it's time to learn about items that make your scrapbook fun to look at. In this chapter I describe the embellishments (that's the fancy word we use for things that make a scrapbook look pretty) that are most popular to the beginning scrapbooker—pre-illustrated accents. Pre-illustrated accents are illustrated, cut-out pieces such as stickers, paper dolls, and titles. Some items come in packages pre-cut and require you to put them together, but usually accents are readily available to use—just glue and add on to your page.

In this chapter, I talk about different scrapbook accents, where to find them, and how to use them to give your books personality—*your* personality. Although accents are not necessary for archival scrapbooking, they are what make scrapbooking fun. So read on to find what kind of accents are available.

Sticky Points

Be warned that this is also the part that can add a lot of cost to scrapbooks. When you go into a scrapbook store, there will be many stickers, paper dolls, titles, and other pre-illustrated accents to tempt you!

Title It

Titling your layouts is a traditional design tool that is used over and over in scrapbooking. The title defines the layout and starts the story. You can spend quite a bit of time hand-drawing your titles or cutting out those great template letters. One way to get the illustrated look is to use the large variety of pre-illustrated titles out there. The topics available range from holidays to sports; you're sure to find something to suit your needs.

Many companies that create titles offer matching paper that coordinates perfectly. You can use the title, then mat or color block with the coordinating pattern paper.

Note how the paper coordinates with the title.

Also available is a title with a coordinated border and accents all on one piece of paper.

This title looks like it's hand drawn.

The accent and title came from the same piece.

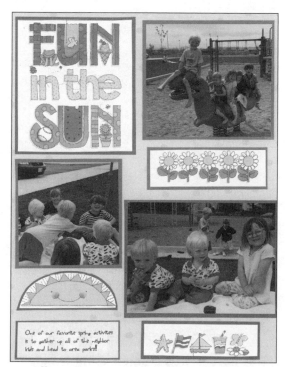

All accents came on the same card.

Also available are sheets that have just titles on them and have separately sold sheets with matching accents.

The "Shoot" title and accents on this page coordinate—they were created from the same company, sold on two different sheets.

One of my favorite companies is My Mind's Eye. They make a line of *accents* that mix and match, and they have everything from titles to pattern paper.

Words for Posterity

An **accent** is a decorative item that is not essential to your scrapbook. Stickers, frames, and paper dolls are a few examples of accents.

All pieces match and are purchased separately so you buy just the pieces you need.

From the Archives

Mrs. Grossman's Paper Company started in a 50-square-foot playhouse. Mrs. Grossman had only two employees (her 12-year-old son and his friend). In a little more than 20 years, it grew to become one of the most popular sticker companies and now employs more than 150 people!

Over the Border

In design, borders define space in useful and decorative ways. Borders help keep designs contained and organized. Wallpaper borders are a great example; they are often featured with wallpaper designs because they separate and unite patterns. Borders are appealing and comforting to the eye. They are used in scrapbooks to decorate pages, but also to tie patterns and themes together and define space on pages. Borders are simple to create and can give your book a great look. A border can be anything from a solid coordinating color to a combination of journaling, hand-drawn curlicues, or stickers. The borders shown below are made from pre-illustrated materials. As you review them, make a mental note of how you can create your own from scratch using these as a guide.

This border was created using a simple sticker pre-made border.

This layout uses the border on different parts of the page to create interest.

You can purchase stickers that have more than one border sticker. Try using it for the border and for framing photos or journaling.

To use individual stickers to create a border, follow these four steps:

1. Once you have selected your pictures, select the stickers you want to use to reinforce your photo story.

2. Decide on the placement of your border.

3. Place the stickers where you want them.

4. Connect the sticker designs somehow, either by overlapping the stickers or by connecting them with hand-drawn doodles.

Don't feel you have to use pre-printed borders just at the bottom of the page. Try using them on top, on the side, or in the corner.

Here is a pre-illustrated border that demands it go on the bottom of the page.

This simple border sticker ties the page together.

Cut It Out the Easy Way

Many scrapbook stores give their customers access to their die-cut machines, often free of charge if you use paper purchased at the store. If you don't have access to a die-cut machine, don't despair! You can buy the designs precut for a small price. And while precut designs don't have as large a range of color options, you can still purchase some great die cuts. Remember, if you want to layer these, buy more than one color.

Die-cut designs are cut from paper. The process begins when a die is inserted into a die-cut machine and pressed onto paper, cutting and perforating it into a design or shape. Die cuts can be used to embellish your page.

When planning on die cutting at your local scrapbook store, plan ahead to get the most out of your trip:

♦ If you have a chance to cut your own dies, get to the store early so you can choose your paper.

♦ Die cutting goes more quickly and takes less effort if you use more than one piece of paper at a time in the machine.

♦ Go to the store with a list of colors and patterns in mind (or better yet, written down) so you won't waste time during your appointment.

♦ Place the paper in the die with the pattern side down to ensure a clean edge on the finished product.

Die-cut machines and dies were originally made for use in schools. Teachers used the fun shapes for decorating their classroom boards, art projects, and classroom borders. Now there are two large die-cut companies that sell the machines and the dies. Many designs are now created just for the scrapbooker.

Now that you know about die cuts, let me give you some of my favorite ways to use them:

♦ Use die cuts as embellishments on your layout.

♦ Use die cuts as a journaling block.

♦ Die cuts can be used to create a title for your page.

♦ Cut the dies into a wreath or make one by layering the dies.

♦ Use the jumbo dies to create great title pages for your books.

♦ Use one design and turn it into something else. For example, if you have a pumpkin die cut, cut it in red, add some small vines and leaves, and presto—you have a garden-ripe tomato that would be perfect for your harvest pages.

♦ Use small die cuts for great borders.

♦ Combine them with other accents. For example, place sticker apples in a die-cut bushel.

Some scrapbook stores create their own custom die cuts, based on what customers say they want. The stores send the designs to die-cut companies and have them prepare special dies. This way, shapes that are interesting to scrapbookers are available.

Framed

One of my favorites on the scene of great products just for scrapbooking are Frame-Ups. These are hand-illustrated precut frames that fit pictures sized 3×5 and 4×6. The colors coordinate with all of the scrapbooking products already available and add instant flair to your page.

Trim your frame to fit your needs.

Other companies have come out with specifically decorated frames—when you use these on your page you don't need to add much more.

This frame's illustration defines the purpose of the layout.

Anna Griffin, an elegant scrapbooking paper company, created frames that coordinate with its exclusive designs.

Use sticker frames for a quick and easy page.

This delicate sticker frame works with the little girl photo.

Color Me Mine: Paper Dolls

Everywhere you turn people are personalizing everything from their license plates to their websites. Such is the case with paper dolls. The availability to personalize this timeless accent is endless.

Maybe your family ethnic background doesn't match the readily available selection. Well, there is a product for you. You can purchase from Cock-a-Doodle Design the page bodies and purchase separately page heads with different skin colors and hair colors and a coordinating skin color marker to color in the shown body parts. This is a fabulous concept! Go to Cock-a-Doodle Design's website to see how these are used (www.cockadoodledesign.com).

This doll is ready to go.

This layout features an oversize sticker kid.

The paper dolls in this layout were person-alized with skin and hair color.

Pick up a paper doll in a bag that requires minimal gluing to personalize that fishing page.

These paperkins come not only with clothes to dress the doll, but also with coordinating elements such as the sun and clouds.

Punches

Punches refer to the tools used to create small shapes as well as the shapes created by the punches.

Punches come in several different types, and each type of punch has many different patterns:

- ◆ **Basic shapes.** Circles, hearts, and trees
- ◆ **Silhouettes.** This punch cuts out the sur-rounding space so its shape is outlined
- ◆ **Corners.** These are designed to cut the corners of your pages
- ◆ **Borders.** Thinner punches used to create borders along the bottom of your page

This stick kitpaper doll came with different cloth options to personalize.

Sticky Points

If your punch jams up, punch through a couple layers of waxed paper to lubricate it. To sharpen it, do the same thing with some fine grade sandpaper. Some of the intricate punches get paper stuck in them from time to time; you can use a small crochet hook to get it out.

Some of my favorite uses for punches are the following:

◆ As accents on page.

◆ As a border on page.

◆ As a frame around pictures.

◆ To create a different design. You can make different punches by layering just as you would a die cut. A great punch idea I saw in a punch art book had a house punch cut in half and placed in half of a circle—it looked like Noah's Ark!

◆ Use in your title to add spark; for example, add some star punches to your Fourth of July title page.

Accentuate Your Scrapbook Line

While many of the scrapbooking supplies we use are borrowed from other crafting arenas—rubber stamps and stickers, for example, are stationery items—there are a few items that were created strictly for scrapbooking.

Punch 'Em Out

Perforated punches are fun accents that you punch out and adhere to your page. These make darling embellishments, are sold in books, and are included in some specialty

paper packs. Hot Off the Press sells these punches in many different theme books. These are great and so easy to use—all you do is punch them out and adhere them to your page. If you need help deciding where to put them, check out the included idea page.

These flower punch-outs are perfect.

These accents are just right for this first-day-of-school page.

Stuck on Stickers

I have a friend who can draw any object or scene freehand. With a few strokes of her pen, she adds all sorts of details to her letters, scrapbooks, and cards. I don't have that talent. Besides a happy face and the occasional flower, my ability to draw is minimal. Luckily, I can use stickers to make up for my lack of artistic ability. Stickers are available in so many colors, patterns, shapes, and scenes that you're bound to find one to match any layout. Use a sticker not only to liven up your page, but to tell a better story, which, after all, is the purpose of your scrapbook.

Try framing stickers as done on this page.

If you use *stickers* created specifically for scrapbooks, you can rest assured that the adhesive is safe. But if you purchase stickers designed for other purposes, you need to check them out. Be careful with the stickers that you buy from mass-merchant stores. Some of them may have acidic adhesive that is harmful to your pages. You can always contact the manufacturer or use a pH testing pen to determine if the sticker is safe. In any case, try not to apply the sticker directly to any photo.

> **Words for Posterity**
>
> **Stickers** are adhesive decorative accents ranging in size from a few centimeters to a full page.

Stickers are a great way to restate the theme of your page. If the page looks a little blah, try using a festive sticker to perk it up. You can use anything from simple primary-colored balloons for a birthday page to an Eiffel Tower sticker to go with your honeymoon in Paris photos. The only thing to worry about with stickers is going overboard. I know those stickers are cute, but remember, you are trying to highlight your photos. I see many of my students try to use every single sticker that comes with the sheet in their layouts. My advice to them? Stickers randomly placed on a page are not nearly as appealing as stickers placed with purpose.

These 3-D stickers create a magical look.

Shortcuts

To title your page, try using some of the sticker letters that are available. They come in a large variety of colors as well as designs—match the style of lettering to the theme of your page.

Wondering where to find all these stickers? Scrapbook stores sell a big variety, and new stickers come out all the time. One secret is to make friends with the store staff so they can alert you when they get a new shipment. Don't forget to check out sticker catalogs and websites, many of which feature ideas of how to use them—a great way to get those creative juices flowing. One of my favorite online sticker sites is Sticker Planet at www.stickerplanet.com. They have a wide selection of stickers and a brilliant website with lots of shopping options and ideas. You can order their sticker catalog by calling 1-800-555-8678. Check it out. (See Appendix A for more websites that sell stickers and other accents.)

Before making a sticker purchase, check to see if instructions accompany the stickers. Many stickers are sold with ideas for using them written right on the back. Look for coordinating stationery and pattern paper as well.

Experience has taught me that it's important to buy spare stickers. If you buy too few, it's easy to run out of stickers before you finish a layout. Don't let this happen to you!

Faux Accents

Want the latest look of 3-D accents without the lumps? Try accents from Fresh Cuts or Ivy Cottage Creations. These unique accents are the newest in the scrapbooking world and give you the homemade look without all the work.

This Easter layout was a breeze to create, yet looks handmade.

Shortcuts

Handmade Scraps makes embellishments that have color added to them so they have a layered die-cut look without all of the work.

Words for Posterity

Perforated punches are shapes that the scrapbooker can use as embellishments on a page. They are simple to use—just punch out on the perforations and apply to your page.

Because *cutouts* are available in many of the popular Disney characters, like Mickey Mouse, Winnie the Pooh, and Simba from the *Lion King*, these are a favorite for kids' scrapbooks. My son Nathan is a big fan of Winnie the Pooh and loves to look at his pictures on the Pooh paper.

Words for Posterity

Cutouts are designs that usually coordinate with pattern paper and are meant to be cut out. They don't have perforated edges.

Shortcuts

If you like the idea of *photo corners* but not the look, try clear photo mounting corners. Available in many different sizes, they are an invisible way to mount a photo to a page.

Words for Posterity

Photo corners are used to adhere photos in scrapbooks and photo albums without applying adhesive directly to the photo. Many scrapbookers like photo corners because photos can be removed from them without any damage.

The Least You Need to Know

◆ Accents give your pages a polished (and fun!) touch.

◆ Be on the lookout for new stickers, punchouts, and cutouts to coordinate with the theme of your pages. Remember to highlight your photographs, and be careful not to overwhelm them.

◆ You may be able to use a store's die-cut machine to customize these accents.

◆ Seasonal pages look great with coordinating page toppers or title sheets.

◆ Photo corners aren't just for old-fashioned books—they come in colors and clear.

In This Part

Part 3

Essential Skills to Complete Those Albums

Scrapbooking your family photos will enrich your life in many ways. In this part you will learn skills that will help make your scrapbooking experience successful. Enjoy the brief overview on photography that will give you tips on everything from selecting film to selecting a camera. Also read about creating a fun and inviting work environment whether you're working from your kitchen table or from your own workspace. Finally, one important category in scrapbooking is the use of words to tell your photo story. Read the chapter on journaling to learn what to journal, where to journal, and how to get started!

In This Chapter

◆ Making your pictures better—camera and film choices and tips for taking terrific shots

◆ Deciding what kind of scrapbook you want to make

◆ Organizing and sorting pictures and mementos

◆ Short- and long-term storage for photos, souvenirs, and negatives

Photography 101: Taking and Organizing Terrific Pictures

Photographs are the heart of most scrapbooks. Even without embellishments of any kind, photos tell a story. In this chapter, you'll learn tips on how to take terrific pictures. The process isn't mysterious, and it is amazing to me the difference well-taken photos make in a scrapbook. We'll cover things like camera, film choice, and composing photographs to get the best possible pictures.

This chapter also covers important information on storing, filing, and sorting your pictures in ways that make the most sense. I know many people who want to scrapbook but don't know where to start. My mom told me, "I have too many pictures and documents and souvenirs to organize them. I'm just going to leave them all in boxes, and when I'm gone, you can take care of them." (Thanks, Mom!) Whether you have one hundred photos to work with or one thousand, follow these steps for gathering and sorting your photos, negatives, and other memorabilia. And for those of you who have very old photos to work with, I have included special instructions because these photos are easily damaged and need special care.

Choose Your Weapon

The two most popular types of cameras are "point-and-shoot" and "single lens reflex" (SLR) cameras, which both use 35mm film. Digital cameras are also becoming increasingly popular. The one you choose depends basically on how much control you would like to have over your images versus how easy it is to take pictures.

◆ Point-and-shoot cameras are extremely easy to use. Point the camera at whatever you're taking a picture of, make sure the flash is on if you need it, and push the button. These cameras usually come with a built-in flash, focus automatically, and advance film automatically. These cameras are light and relatively inexpensive.

◆ Single lens reflex (SLR) cameras are somewhat more complicated to use but allow you to control your images in a way that is impossible with point-and-shoot cameras. Although you can buy SLRs that are fully automatic and as easy to use as a point-and-shoot, you can also set most SLRs to manual. Manual controls allow you to focus the camera yourself, control the exposure duration, and set the camera's *aperture* wider or smaller. You can also change lenses on an SLR camera, something you cannot do with a point-and-shoot.

Words for Posterity

The **aperture** is the opening in a camera that lets in light. The aperture opens and closes when you snap a picture. When light hits the film, an image is made. Setting the aperture wider allows more light into the camera, while setting it smaller allows less light in.

◆ Digital cameras allow you to snap images that are stored directly onto computer disks. There is no film to develop, and the pictures can be viewed on a computer and then printed. Digital camera controls are similar to SLR cameras and produce high-quality images. If you have a computer and a high-quality color printer and money is no object, this may be an option for you.

◆ Polaroids are *not* a good choice for preservation because the processing chemicals are retained in the finished prints. Use this for a fun second camera, but not to record your family's history.

Capture the Moment—Choosing the Right Film Speed

A film's *speed* tells you how sensitive the film is to light and is indicated by an ASA (or sometimes an ISO) number on the film's container. The higher the ASA number, the more sensitive the film is to light. What that means practically is that slower film speeds (ASA 64–125) are good to use outdoors in bright light and higher speeds (ASA 400–800) can be used in lower-light situations.

Words for Posterity

Film speed refers to a film's sensitivity to light. Lower-speed films are less sensitive—use these on a bright, sunny day. Higher-speed films are more sensitive—use these in low-light situations.

From the Archives

Before the invention of 35mm film, photographs were made one at a time on large, heavy glass plates. Each plate was coated with light-sensitive chemicals just before the photograph was taken and then developed right away. Today's film, though much smaller and lighter, works on the same principle—it is covered with emulsion that is light-sensitive. When light hits the film through the camera's lens, it creates an image. The film must be processed to see the image (that makes a negative) and then printed onto photographic paper.

In addition, faster film speeds can capture movement without blurring (good to know when you are taking pictures of your child's softball game), but may lose detail and produce a grainy print. Slower-speed film will let you capture fine details in portraits but is not good for action shots. Following are recommendations for using different film speeds. Very slow film (ASA 25–32) can be purchased but may be hard to find and is not generally useful to the average picture taker.

- **Medium speed (ASA 64–125).** Recommended uses: Great for taking pictures of a newborn where there is plenty of light (if the baby moves around there will be some blurring on the photos—this isn't all bad because it conveys a sense of movement). Prop the baby on a blanket on the lawn, hold the camera steady, and snap away.

- **Faster speed (ASA 200–400).** Recommended uses: Good for situations where there isn't a lot of available light, such as early evening, or using indoors in a bright room without a flash. Fast-speed film can also capture movement without blurring.

- **ASA 200** is an all-purpose film speed. Take it along to the beach, to the park, to any outdoor, medium- to bright-sun activity. Its medium-fast speed will allow you to capture detail without much blurring.

- Use **ASA 400** in low light or situations where there's a lot of movement (good for sports events or snapping the kids running around under the sprinkler). Keep in mind that some of these pictures may have a grainy quality, especially if you make enlargements.

Shortcuts

Consider asking employees of photo labs to recommend brands of film—a lab in a mall might develop on average 30 to 80 rolls each day. Without even knowing it, those employees become experts in the types of film. So ask lots of questions. What they like to develop should be the film in your camera.

- **Very fast speed (ASA 800–1600).** Recommended uses: Good for extreme low-light conditions, such as a wedding indoors when you don't have a flash. Film this fast can let you take pictures that would otherwise be impossible, but pictures may be grainy even if they are not enlarged. You can try using ASA 1600 in near total darkness as long as there is some available light source, such as a candle, a lamp, fireworks, or even moonlight (on an SLR, set your camera to a long exposure).

It's a good idea to carry a few different kinds of film with you—weather conditions and light can change, and it would be a shame to miss a great shot because your film can't handle the existing light conditions.

Sticky Points

Always remember to check the expiration date on your film—after that date, film likely will not perform well.

It's also a good idea to consider getting your pictures developed at a photo lab—the difference in the quality of pictures that you'll get back versus pictures developed at the corner drug store can be tremendous. Photo labs are more expensive, but they are the best choice for developing important pictures. You'll be pleased by the results.

Taking Great Portraits

Creating wonderful portraits is a challenge for any photographer. Great portrait photographers speak of a "moment of truth" that reveals a person's character. Sometimes, all you need is a quick snap that captures a spontaneous moment; other times, you'll want to be more careful and try to capture a person's mood and character.

♦ **Lighting.** The most important element in a picture. The most flattering light for portraits comes from a bit above and off to the side. Other lighting can be used for interesting effects, such as creating silhouettes.

♦ **Posing.** Make sure the people or person is relaxed. If your subject is nervous, chat with the person to put him or her at ease. If you are shooting a group, don't make them stand rigidly; let them relax into their poses.

♦ **Props/background.** You can use these to create an interesting effect. Sometimes, you'll have to make do with what is around; other times, you'll be able to pick these to create a theme.

♦ **Direction.** Head-on shots can appear stiff and unnatural, while placing a subject off to the side might be more relaxed. Profile shots can be interesting and dramatic.

♦ **Position.** When taking pictures of kids, keep in mind that they are small and short—so don't be afraid to move in!

These shots make creative use of props.

Top Ten Tips for Taking Terrific Pictures

Eliott Erwitt, world-renowned photographer, once said, "All the technique in the world doesn't compensate for the inability to notice." The best way to improve your photographs is to work on becoming a world-class noticer— watch out for interesting images, and your photography will improve. A photographer friend of mine suggested these 10 ways for anybody to take better pictures.

Shortcuts

Try using props to accentuate the character of the person whose portrait you are taking. For instance, if you are taking shots of a good friend who plays the violin, consider posing her with the instrument or against a background of musical notes—not anything too distracting, but something that shows who the subject is.

1. **Change your point of view.** Don't always plop down right in front of your subject. Try changing your angle, tilting your camera, getting on one knee, or standing on a ladder. If your camera has auto focus, don't even look through the viewfinder. Guesstimate and be surprised at what turns out.

2. **Get closer.** Get in close to your subjects. People are sometimes afraid to get up close, resulting in a subject being a mere dot in the photo.

Make sure your subjects aren't dots in your pictures—get in close.

3. **But not too close.** On the other hand, there's such a thing as too close—hey, it's a camera, not a medical probe. This happens most often with newborn babies—remember that most auto focus cameras require you to be about three or four feet away. Any closer, and your baby is one very cute blur.

4. **Follow the law of thirds.** Here's an old photographer's trick—put your subject in the left or right third of the frame instead of dead center. These compositions are more pleasing to the eye.

5. **Compose as you snap.** You can easily crop photographs after they are developed, but try to frame the image in your mind's eye as you are taking it. Make sure all the elements are within the lines of the camera's viewfinder, and take a picture that already contains the balance, subjects, and shapes you want.

6. **Get a 35mm camera.** If you own a disk or 110 camera, it's time to toss it out. The negatives from disk and 110 cameras are so small they can't help but take poor pictures. A cheap 35mm can be purchased for less than $40—they're not the best cameras, but if you're on a budget, they're great. First learn to take good pictures, then graduate to a better camera.

7. **Use your flash outdoors.** Ever take a photo of your family underneath a tree and notice that half of the faces are covered in shadow? A flash used outdoors is called "fill flash" and can reduce this problem. If you are taking pictures of people outside, try using your flash on every picture (usually your subject needs to be less than 15 feet away).

8. **Take some candid shots.** It's so intrusive to constantly ask people to stop what they're doing to "say cheese." Candid pictures capture people's expressions and activities wonderfully. And if you do take posed photos, take them quickly—get the flash ready, make sure the film is advanced, and the lens cap is off.

9. **Be mindful of your backgrounds.** For instance, when taking photos of a newborn baby, try not to pose the baby on a solid-color blanket. Unless you are getting your film developed by a custom developer, the baby will take on the color of the blanket. In any shot, ask yourself if the background will flatter or detract from your subject.

10. **Take lots of pictures.** If a professional photographer gets one picture they are happy with on a roll of 36, they are ecstatic. Follow the photographer's rule and carry your camera around all the time. A picture may be worth a thousand words, but if you don't take the photo when the moment arrives, it's worth only one word—"Darn."

Get It All Together— Establishing a Gathering Place

So you've taken a ton of pictures, and you have even more sitting around in boxes. Before you rush from room to room, unearthing all your family treasures, you need to establish a gathering place.

If you have an entire room for your scrapbook project, great. Stash everything in there. Or find a corner where you can leave your photos for a few days while you are organizing them. In my house, this is the floor on my side of the bed, but if you have a table or countertop that you can use, great. If you don't have

small kids or pets running around, go ahead and leave them anywhere they won't be disturbed by drafts or wind. Just be sure that they aren't in the way of heating vents, as this is damaging to photos.

Now, go through your house looking for photos and souvenirs. If you are well organized, this shouldn't take long, but, if you're like my sister, you have five or six places where you stash important items. I still remember the thrill of discovering my long-lost program from my eighth grade viola recital. Looking at it brought back the excitement I felt at receiving a superior rating for a piece a group of us did in junior high. Suddenly, I am there playing the viola, and I am winning all over again. This is a great memory for me.

Sticky Points

Because photographs can be damaged by sunlight, keep the room dark if possible by closing the blinds or drawing the curtains.

Call up your extended family to see if they have photos you'd be interested in. Look through your journals and diaries for documents, such as birth certificates, death certificates, school records, and other things you'll want copies of.

Sticky Points

If you are working with very old albums that are tearing apart, handle pictures gently and try not to move them around or leave them exposed when you aren't examining them. It isn't a bad idea to wear photo gloves to handle these, and watch out for dust.

Look to these sources for photos and other mementos that you, or people close to you, might have stashed away:

- ◆ Closets
- ◆ Mixed with school projects (this is often where I have found the class pictures that I forgot to take out and place with photos)
- ◆ From grandparents
- ◆ Hawaii pictures from the couple you went with
- ◆ Cedar chest
- ◆ Other relatives
- ◆ Your children's friends' parents
- ◆ Your favorite photo developing lab— maybe you forgot to pick up some film
- ◆ Old family friends

Shortcuts

Don't overlook the history that goes along with your old photos. As you are looking through these scrapbooks with your family, record their memories of the pictures and events either by taking notes or by recording the conversations.

Treat Old Photos and Mementos Gently

Most of us have photos that have been improperly stored. Photos of mine that were once stored in magnetic albums are yellowing and faded. And other old photos and mementos that have been stored in the bottom of closets or in drawers can show their age. What can you do about this? I've gathered advice and information for you.

Old Photo Albums

If you're working with old photo albums where the pictures are fastened with photo corners, you're in luck. Usually all you have to do is remove the photo; the adhesive will often have already worn off some, if not all, of the corners. If the pictures are brittle, proceed carefully. Consider copying them so you won't damage the originals. Take them to a photo preservationist if you want an expert opinion. If you decide to copy your old photographs, beware that some copy machines are too hot for photos and can damage them, and make sure the one you use is safe.

Shortcuts

Use a soft, clean cloth to wipe off dirt and fingerprints. Do not use facial tissues or paper towels—these items have microscopic fibers that could scratch your photos.

Magnetic Albums

So-called "magnetic" albums are destructive to your photos because the adhesives emit harmful chemicals. If you've got photos in these types of albums, get them out as soon as possible. Here are a few different ways to remove them. Some photos are really stubborn, so you might have to try several techniques.

- ◆ Pry up a corner of the photo with a table knife or other flat object. Aim a blow dryer set on low under the photo to loosen the glue until you can remove the photo.

Shortcuts

It's a good idea to keep a wax pencil or photographic marker with you as you remove photos to jot down notes on the back of the pictures. Any original captions should be recorded.

◆ Slip some waxed dental floss under the photo. Use a sawing motion to loosen the glue.

◆ Try the adhesive remover Undu. This dissolves the glue used in magnetic photo albums.

◆ If all else fails, see a photo expert. Remember, you don't want to be rough with your photos—you can ruin them!

Adhesive remover will become your new best friend if you are removing old photos.

Restoring Old Documents

If old documents are soiled, you can try cleaning them off using small bits of an eraser. If the documents have any rips, use a special document tape that is available through archival sources. Do your best to handle these items carefully. If all else fails, take the documents to a copy store.

Remember to store these precious documents flat with a piece of acid-free paper in between each document rather than standing them up in files; this prevents them from bending. If you are going to use these documents in your albums, make sure they are in sheet protectors to prevent further damage.

What "Sort" of Stuff Have You Found?

Now think about the type of scrapbook album you are working on. Are you doing a master one for yourself? Are you doing one for each of your children and grandchildren? Are you working on a family Christmas album? What if you just want to organize all your photos and use a select few in one special scrapbook? The important thing is to decide what your ultimate goal is before you begin sorting.

Shortcuts

Use copies of documents and certificates as background paper in your scrapbook.

Step 1—Make It Manageable

Divide the pictures into manageable increments. If you are working on a collection of 40 years' worth of photos, start by dividing them into decades, then work on each decade separately.

Pile the pictures into boxes that are labeled by decade and divide each of those boxes into years within that decade. If you only have three or four years' worth of photos, you can sort first by year, then by season, and so on.

Step 2—Who *Are* These People?

Step 1 works perfectly if every picture you have is nicely labeled with the year it was taken and a neat narrative about who is in the picture, where they are, and what they are doing. But this is unlikely—if we were all this organized, our photos would've been in albums long ago! Figuring out the year and what is going on in the photos is half the fun, especially if you haven't looked at the pictures in years. What can help you figure out when the pictures were taken?

◆ Check the background of the picture for clues—maybe you can just make out a banner in the background that says "Happy New Year 1977." (Perfect for the first picture in that album!)

◆ What type of clothes is everyone wearing? Coats for winter, swimsuits for summer, bell bottoms in the early seventies (fashions can often help determine what year it is, as well as the season).

◆ How old are the children in the pictures? If you can figure out even approximately how old the children in the picture are, you can probably figure out the year.

◆ Who is everyone hanging out with? If the photo is of you, say, with your friends Sharon and Marie from an old job, that'll help you guess when the picture was taken.

◆ Who are these people? If you're having trouble identifying some of the faces in a picture, enlist your family—maybe your brother can recall an old friend from your high school years.

Step 3—Pictures and Keepsakes Go Together

Finally, all the photos are sorted according to the chronological order. The next step is to decide what type of memorabilia you want to include. I like to store my mementos in separate containers. One idea to help remember which memento goes with which pictures is to make a corresponding note or tag to place with the photos that corresponds to the era or event the memento comes from (just don't use sticky back notes because the adhesive is damaging to your photo).

Let's say you have pictures of your honeymoon trip to Spain, and you find ticket stubs for the romantic train ride you and your spouse took from Madrid to Barcelona. Note this on a piece of cardstock that you file with the photographs. Store the tickets in a separate container in the same chronological order as the photographs. When you are ready to make the album, you'll see the reminder among the pictures and find the old tickets in your file.

Shortcuts

There are many ways mementos can be sorted—chronologically, but also by topic (such as sports, awards, trips, pets), and by person (have a box labeled with someone's name and keep together all the mementos and souvenirs that have to do with him or her).

Step 4—Focus on a Theme

The next step is to determine the type of album you are creating.

My next-door neighbor decided she wanted to do scrapbooks for each of her grown children. She spent a couple of weeks gathering photos, another couple of weeks sorting the pictures, and then became frustrated. Because there were so many good pictures of the family and many of the photos were of all the kids together, she couldn't decide which child should get which photos.

Shortcuts

When you are making multiple albums of the same time period, consider creating one master page and having it copied for all of the albums.

If you come across this problem, you have a few options. You can divide the pictures up evenly and just give child A different ones from child B and C, and so forth. Another option is to copy the photos and create different layouts for all of the children. While this is time-consuming, it is nice to create a one-of-a-kind scrapbook for each child.

Another good idea is to create a *master family album*. This kind of book contains all the family pictures, including school photos, portraits, family vacations, and everything pertaining to your family. These are best organized in chronological order. The nice thing about these albums is everything is in one place. You are not creating duplicate pages, and none of the children feel left out.

Words for Posterity

A **master family album** contains pictures of everyone in the family and family documents, typically in chronological order.

Theme albums, or simple scrapbooks, are also popular. Just recently, in one of my classes, a mother and her two daughters were working on a theme album for the girls' father. They combined their efforts in gathering the photos and put the album together in less than four weeks. He loves to fish with his grandchildren, and he loves to take pictures. So they surprised him for Father's Day with a 50-page album of him fishing through the years and ending up with the last 15 pages of him fishing with his grandkids. After they gathered as many pictures as they could, they went through them together and sorted the photos according to year and category: fishing as a child, fishing with friends, fishing trips to Montana, and so forth. Each family member then took a couple of sections and worked on them. Later, they got together to put on the finishing touches and compile all the sections. It was a wonderful gift and a fun project.

Words for Posterity

A **theme album** is a scrapbook devoted to one idea. Some popular theme albums focus on birthdays, weddings, and school days.

They're Sorted—Now Where Can You Keep Them?

Two photo storage options exist: long-term and temporary.

Short-term or temporary storage usually is not safe for photographs to stay in for too long, but pictures will usually do all right for a little while, say a month or so. For short-term storage, I like to use plastic shoeboxes for my photos because they are inexpensive, lightweight, and see-through. I use scraps of cardstock to divide my photos into categories.

Since the plastic isn't acid-free, these containers will damage your photos in the long run, so use them only for current projects.

> **Sticky Points**
>
> As convenient as it might seem, refrain from using paper clips, rubber bands, or other office supplies to organize your pictures. These can leave damaging and unattractive imprints on your photographs.

Good long-term storage options:

◆ For projects such as theme albums or ongoing books or for any type of book, use your binders as your storage. Slip the categorized photos in your sheet protectors in the order you want them.

◆ Be on the lookout for photo chests made from acid-free cardboard. These are available in decorator styles and keep your photographs organized and safe.

◆ Some scrapbook stores carry expensive storage items that are made for long-term photo storage. Try www. lastingimpressions.com for a good selection of long-term storage options.

Store Negatives Safely

Negatives last longer than color photographs, so you want to make sure that you store all those slippery negatives in a safe place. You never know when you'll need reprints of lost or ruined pictures.

> **Sticky Points**
>
> Though it's easier to store negatives in the house, it's not advisable. In the case of burglary, flood, or natural disaster, you'll want copies of your precious pictures. It's a good idea to store at least the most precious ones in a safe deposit box or in a fireproof safe at a family member's house.

The easiest way to store negatives is in negative holders. These are similar to photo sleeves, but they have pockets sized to hold an individual strip of negatives. Many of them include space to label the negatives (a good idea) and have holes punched along their sides. Place these pocket pages in an album, and you're set.

Buying tabbed protectors to put in your negative albums will help keep them organized. Place the date of the negatives on the tabs, and you'll have an easier time finding negatives when you need them.

The Least You Need to Know

◆ Photographs are the heart of a scrapbook. Anyone can take better pictures by following a few simple guidelines.

◆ Take your important film to be developed at a good photo lab—you'll be happy with the results.

◆ Enlist friends and relatives to help you gather pictures and mementos and identify people and eras in your pictures.

◆ Sort photographs and souvenirs according to the type of scrapbook you want to make. Possibilities include master family albums and celebrations of special events, like holidays, birthdays, trips, and family gatherings.

◆ Be gentle with old photographs and albums and figure out good storage for photographs, keepsakes, documents, and negatives until you are ready to use them.

In This Chapter

◆ Using souvenirs in your scrapbook

◆ Making souvenirs safe with deacidification products

◆ Neat projects for saving keepsakes

One of our activites was making friendship bracelets for each other—I wear my favorite one and have saved the rest in this pocket.
March 2002

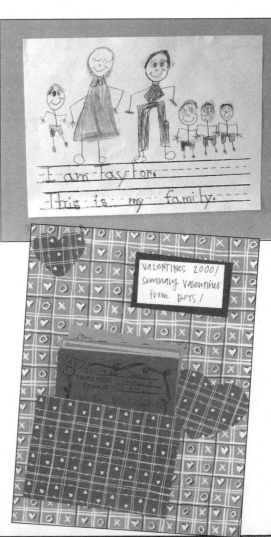

Chapter 11

Saving Souvenirs

Souvenirs—we all have them. And we hate to part with them. After all, who wants to throw away your six-year-old's drawing of the family cat or the tickets from your junior prom? What about the program from your college graduation? Well, you don't have to throw them away nor do you have to shove them in that shoebox crammed under your bed because there is a better way.

But you may have some questions about saving keepsakes: What items are good to save? How do I save them? And of course, where on earth can I keep them? You'll find the answers to these and more questions in this chapter.

Holding On to Yesterday

Tickets, programs, maps and the like are often printed on low-grade, highly acidic papers. Despite all your efforts, souvenirs can threaten the archival environment you've worked so hard to create for your photographs. Because they are so important to the story that you are telling, you must include them, but how can you make them safe and lasting?

Dropping the Acid

Thanks to some incredible products, this is now a fairly simple task. Sprays on the market, called deacidification sprays, actually neutralize the acid in your mementos, making them safe to use in your scrapbook. To use these sprays, flatten and spread out the items you want to spray. Keep items as close together as possible without overlapping to use the spray most effectively. Go ahead and spray on an even coat, covering items but not soaking them. Do not pick up the sprayed items until they are completely dry and then handle them with care so that you don't introduce any more acid to them.

From the Archives

Preserving mementos with photos has always been a favorite pastime of artists and photographers as they have combined pamphlets with photos in an effort to preserve their work.

While these sprays can be expensive, they are a good investment. After all, the items you are preserving are priceless.

Copy and Scan

The other thing you can do is to go to your local photocopy shop and make color copies of the items on acid-free paper. This way you can place the copies in your scrapbook and safely store the originals. You can also reduce or enlarge these color copies to make whatever it is you're including just the right size for your page.

Shortcuts

Need an interesting background for your Halloween pages? Try color copying candy for the background. You can use a tray to place the items in and then copy away.

Color copying isn't just for souvenirs, photos, and documents—you can color copy almost anything. Try copying fabric, your wedding dress, or even flower petals. One of the sweetest baby pages I've seen was created by color copying a portion of a baby blanket and using that for the background to display a picture of baby wrapped in the blanket.

This layout shows the special certificate reduced down small enough for a page, large enough to read.

If you own a *scanner* that is attached to your computer, use it! Besides photos and certificates, you can also scan clothes and other items into your computer and then print them. Try doing this with a blessing or christening gown. Making a scouting album? Scan those merit badge patches and print them out on paper to display alongside the photos.

Words for Posterity

A **scanner** is a device that enables you to copy items for inputting into your computer.

Sticky Points

When scanning in items to use in your scrapbook, the color probably will not be as true as a color copy. For instance, white will tend to have a green tint. Experiment to see what you can get.

Saving Your Budding Picasso's Works of Art

Anyone who has been the recipient of children's artwork knows how precious and heartwarming it is. When children express themselves through art, the results are touching. Here are a few different methods for saving artwork. See which works best for you:

◆ Create albums of your child's artwork. Spray each piece with deacidification spray and place them in a page protector. Put the protectors in an album.

◆ Choose the special pieces to display in a child's chronological scrapbook. Take a photo of him holding his artwork and put it in his scrapbook next to the original.

◆ For oversize art, go to the color copier and have the artwork reduced so that it can fit in your book.

◆ Arrange the artwork on the floor and take photos of your child with it.

◆ Try scanning the pieces into your computer and keep files of the scanned images to keep track on disc.

Here is a layout created from photos of the child while doing her oversize art project.

Your refrigerator is too small—save your child's artwork in a special scrapbook.

Keeping Documementos

If there is a helpful copy shop near where you live, you can have a lot of fun with your certificates, or *documementos*. Try taking in card-size stationery and having the shop print your daughter's birth certificate in the middle. That would make a great page, and you can reduce or enlarge the certificate to fit your needs. Some of the most creative uses of documents I have seen were pages copied from the phone book to show a fun ad or home number.

If you don't want to go to the expense or trouble of deacidifying some ticket stubs or greeting cards, at least make sure that you put them on their own page—not directly next to your pictures. You can also mount them onto buffered cardstock for added protection (and spraying them with deacidifying spray would also make them safe).

This is a great time for pocket pages, too. Create a simple pocket out of two sheets of cardstock to hold items such as Valentine cards or ticket stubs. Don't forget to include all of those love notes from college!

Enjoy the valentines forever in this pocket page designed by Nikki Maw to contain her valentine notes.

Three-Dimensional Memories

Those baby booties your daughter wore when she was three weeks old are too cute to stash in a box somewhere. The same goes for the pet rock you had that your mom kept all these years. Believe it or not, these can be displayed in your scrapbook, too!

There are special pages called 3-D keepsake holders that are three-dimensional pages you can place objects into. Try saving items from your childhood or a favorite vacation. The 3-D pages slip right into your scrapbook and are available for both 8½ × 11 and 12 × 12 albums.

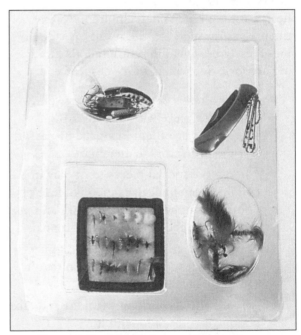

Keep 3-D objects in special pockets.

Memorabilia pockets are another fun way to display souvenirs in your scrapbook. They come in a variety of sizes, from 2 × 2 inches to 8½ × 11 inches. People love to use these for locks of hair, but with a little creativity, you can put in anything: a rosebud from a special bouquet, the key from your first car, or a name tag from that silly summer high school job.

In these 3-D pockets special jewelry is saved from a best friends party.

Sowing Ideas—Make a Special Garden Scrapbook

Flowers are some of nature's most brilliant items and often hold special meaning to people. Here are some ways to preserve flowers in your scrapbooks:

◆ Insert dried and pressed flowers into memorabilia pockets and stick them right on the page.

◆ Color copy petals from a special bouquet or corsage.

◆ Adhere dried and pressed flowers directly to the page and gently place photos around them.

◆ Laminate dried and pressed flowers using an acid-free lamination, such as Xyron.

A lovely project would be to create a scrapbook that covers a year in the life of your garden and incorporates pressed flowers or color copies of flowers and plants. Here are some ideas of how you could go to town (or country!) with this scrapbook:

1. Start making your album during the fall clean-up and bulb-planting season:

   ◆ Title page: You might make a color copy of autumn leaves that you take from your backyard (keep them in a sealed bag on the way to the copy shop to preserve the color because these dry up and crack quickly).

   ◆ Include a diagram of the garden showing all the trees, shrubs, and perennials you've planted.

   ◆ Include journaling about how you planted spring flowering bulbs like tulips, daffodils, and crocuses—and include the pretty packaging of what you've planted.

   ◆ As the days get colder, take pictures of your garden in every stage: the stark beauty of the trees as they lose their leaves, and the way the garden looks in snow. In warmer climates, document what your garden looks like year round. If you live in a cold climate, use the winter to plan what you'd like your garden to include come the spring.

2. When spring comes, note the first flowers you see and take pictures and notes as everything comes into full bloom.

   ◆ You could turn your scrapbook into a gardener's almanac by including gardening tips along with the photographs. You can then refer back to the scrapbook when needed. Notes to include might be planting times, fertilization methods, growth success, where items were purchased, and watering methods.

◆ Include photos and colorful seed packets, clips from gardening catalogs, pictures of friends and family in the garden, your own drawings of flowers, pictures or color copies of prized flowers—and don't forget pictures of you in your gardening hat and gloves!

◆ Keep your book up through the summer, as perennials come into bloom and your garden starts to look lush.

3. When the fall comes, you, your garden, and your scrapbook will have come full circle. Imagine how nice it will be that winter to have a chronicle of your garden in full bloom. And in years to come, it will be wonderful to track the changes in your garden (when the tiny sapling you planted becomes a big apple tree) by looking back at your book.

Treasure Boxes and Time Capsules

Scrapbooks are a great way to collect things to save for posterity, but they do have their limitations (it's kinda hard to slip the teddy bear you loved to bits into a scrapbook). Following are two fun ideas for saving larger souvenirs, important sentimental items, and items for posterity.

Yo! Ho! Ho!—Making a Treasure Box

Creating a treasure box is a great way to compile an ongoing legacy for you and your family. You may not have a building named after you—or a flower, or a street—but everyone has things that tell about who they are. And your treasures don't have to be a pirate's ransom of gold bullion and jewel-encrusted daggers—just personal items that mean a lot to you and will mean a lot to your children.

A treasure box can also be a way of commemorating a loved one and telling their stories. Sadly, I have heard of parents who have buried small children and haven't been able to put any of their possessions away because of painful reminders.

Sticky Points

Although it is not easy to scrapbook difficult times, they are an important part of your history. Be respectful of others' needs, though, and carefully choose what is appropriate to share.

Because we all have different lives and histories, we all want to include different things in our treasure boxes. I am going to share with you some of the items I have saved and what I want to add to my treasure box. My goal in doing this is mainly for posterity—I'd like my children to have tangible items from my life and an explanation for things I have saved. I want them to have a true sense of my life and what happened in it. As you see what is inside my treasure box, jot down what you want to include in yours and set a goal to compile it.

Following are the contents of my treasure box:

◆ Childhood journal. This has bits and pieces of my early teens, along with report cards and letters from friends.

◆ A toy I played with as a baby.

◆ High school yearbook. This is more for the interest of clothing styles and the era than for any sentimental meaning.

◆ College papers. Personal essays and papers written for college courses contain my thoughts at that time.

◆ Wedding dress. Because I have all sons, I'll have it forever.

◆ Matchbook from our honeymoon suite. The first time our names were together on a document.

◆ Maternity dress. Looking at it reminds me of being pregnant, the anticipation and excitement.

◆ Baby outfits from each of my children.

◆ Handmade presents. From love letters from my husband to my children's hand-prints.

◆ Books. I love reading, and I have saved a few books that have been very significant to me.

◆ Letters from my parents.

◆ Documents. Certificates, stories written about me by my family members, cards, and so on.

Time in a Bottle—Making a Time Capsule

To make a *time capsule*, first find a container to seal it in. Make sure it is something that is going to be difficult to break into so you won't be tempted to open it up. Gather together everyone you want to participate, make a list of items you want to enclose, and decide how long you want to lock them up for.

> ### Words for Posterity
>
> A **time capsule** is a container holding historical records or objects that represent the culture that deposited it for preservation. If you make a time capsule and intend to open it up sometime, make sure someone remembers where it is!

Items that would be fun to include in a time capsule are …

◆ Newspapers and magazines detailing current events.

◆ For children, a recording of height and weight.

◆ Listing of favorites, such as music, movies, food to eat, places to go, hobbies, books, and clothes.

◆ Articles of clothing, CDs, something that captures that year.

◆ Photographs of everyone involved.

◆ Baby clothes.

◆ List of goals for the next 20 years.

◆ Family predictions for everyone.

◆ Other predictions.

Include anything that would be significant to you and your family. This is a fun undertaking and makes a great excuse to have a party in 20 years!

The Least You Need to Know

◆ There are deacidification products you can use to save many kinds of souvenirs.

◆ You can also keep mementos in 3-D page protectors or sealed-up packets.

◆ Try color copying documents so that you can include the items in your book without using fragile originals. You can copy anything—try color copying candies for a sweet Halloween page.

◆ Save your child's artwork by making a special scrapbook just for art.

◆ Use the ideas in this chapter to make a year-round garden scrapbook, a treasure box, or a time capsule.

In This Chapter

◆ Write for the kids, for the family, for the future, and most of all, for yourself

◆ Great suggestions on where to write stories

◆ Getting-started exercises for those who need help writing

◆ Leave behind not only the pictures, but the meaning behind them

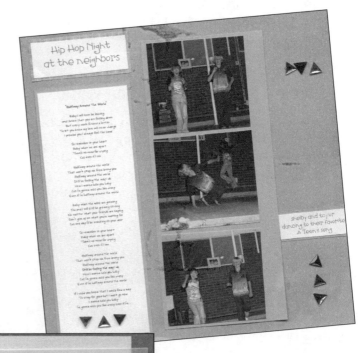

No matter how little money and how few possessions you own, having a dog makes you rich. – Louis Sabin

Chapter 12

Tell Your Story: Journaling in Your Scrapbook

No scrapbook is complete without journaling. Future readers of the scrapbook won't recognize all the faces and will need names, dates, and details. You can write as much or as little as you like in your scrapbook, but you must write something! If you're wondering how to get started, read this chapter for guidelines, tips, and a few ideas to make journaling fun. You can include all kinds of writing in your book, like poetry, stories, jokes, quotes—anything!

The Who, What, When, Where, and Why

What you write in your scrapbook depends a lot on what type of book you're working on. If you're doing a baby book for your daughter, you will probably have all sorts of feelings and memories you want to record; the way you felt when you first laid eyes on her, who received her first smile, and the day she took her first step. But if you're working on an album with pictures of your grandparents, you might not have as many details to include.

For your everyday albums, remember to record the who, what, when, why, and where of your pictures.

◆ Who is in the pictures is an important place to start. Record both first and last names, especially of people who aren't in your family. In the years to come, you may not remember their last names.

◆ What is important because it explains what you are doing and helps the reader to understand the pictures.

◆ When is a must to record so you can look back and not drive yourself crazy because you can't remember when you went to Uncle Jack's cookout. This helps to establish your family history. Every summer, we go to Jackson Hole with my husband's family, and my kids love to look at pictures of us sitting in front of my favorite restaurant. Always include the date somewhere on your page.

◆ Where is a must to include because someday you will forget where you were that year. Give as much detail as possible, especially on trips. A great idea is to include restaurant and hotel locations. Make sure to write down the address. Another great addition is to take pictures of signs or landmarks that add to the story.

◆ Why are you wearing the same shirt in all your pregnant pictures? Why is your cat sitting on top of the refrigerator? Why is your mom wearing a hat made out of a paper plate on her head? The "whys?" (and the "why on earths?") tell much of the story—don't leave them out.

Include the Sublime and the Ridiculous

Make sure to include any interesting stories about the photos. I remember when my husband and I were in a group shot for a magazine article illustrating different types of jobs. I was the mom holding a small child. At the time, I was a few months pregnant, and by the time we were all settled and ready to take the picture, my son had had it. So in the picture, I have a very odd expression on my face because I had to go to the bathroom, my 18-month-old was squirming, and I was very anxious to leave. My family finds this story about that picture very humorous.

The journaling on this layout recounts the basic details of the day's events, who attended, where we were, and why we all came together.

The reader is drawn to the story to discover why this little girl is sitting in the middle of an antique quilt.

Shortcuts

When traveling, take some time to jot down the events and fun times you want to remember. Have your notepad on hand when you're compiling those vacation pictures to help you remember the details.

Jog Your Memories

What if you don't have pictures of important events in your life? This has happened to all of us, whether you forgot the camera, or you were so caught up in the event that taking pictures was not on your mind—until later when you regretted it. You can still record these events in your scrapbooking through journaling. You don't need to have a picture; just write the story down and place it on some fun paper, and you have a nice recollection of the event.

A scrapbook can give modest mothers a chance to brag about their children's accomplishments. You can include a picture of your toddler, his or her age, and current vocabulary. Show your child holding a favorite book and write down the words she recited from the story. When my son Justin was three, he began a love affair with dinosaurs. It would make a great page to show this three-year-old with his favorite dinosaurs and listing all the names of the ones he could say. Your child could also attempt a little journaling himself by writing right in the book.

From the Archives

Do you want to record the voice of your children reading their favorite story? Get the Memory Button. It has a digital recording capability and fits right on your scrapbook page.

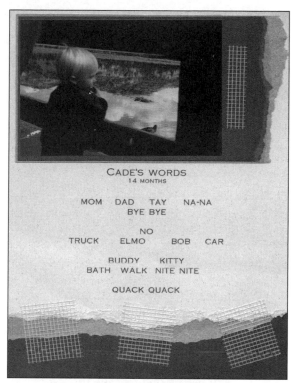

Here is a layout highlighting my son Caden's vocabulary.

So Maybe You're Not Hemingway ... You Still Have a Story to Tell

Some people like to make writing as much a focus of their books as the pictures. Want to tell a story but aren't sure where to start? Here are some exercises to loosen up the storyteller in you.

The Setup, the Meat, and the Caboose

When recounting a story or event, use the three following parts as guidelines to get the information organized:

◆ **Part 1—The setup.** This is the who, when, where of the photo or story.

◆ **Part 2—The meat.** The what, the details of the story.

◆ **Part 3—The caboose, the why.** The significance of the story or why this is funny to you or your family. If you want to make a point with this story, this is the place.

Use humor when sharing stories if appropriate. Add more detail than you think is necessary—you won't believe what you will forget. Whether it is a paragraph or a page, this information is crucial to a scrapbook. This way, you will be the one to have the last word.

Shortcuts

Try keeping a small notebook with you at all times so that when you are waiting in the doctor's office or watching soccer games, you can outline or jot down funny stories that you want to include in your scrapbook. When you start doing your pages, pull out the notebook to jog your memory.

Try Analysis

If you still have a difficult time remembering what is going on during that time, try photo memory therapy. To help you remember certain events, look through your photographs. These will help jog your memories and help you think of things to include in your writing. Try asking yourself a few questions about the photo to get you thinking.

◆ Why did I take a picture of this person, thing, or event?

◆ Who is in the photo and what is my relationship to them?

◆ Is there anything funny or interesting going on that the photo doesn't show?

◆ When was this photo taken?

◆ What were my relationships with these people like?

The only mistake you can make is to feel that you're incapable of writing down events and feelings—the more you write, the better. Keep on, and it will get easier. Use simple, everyday language when recounting an event. Write down what you remember from specific events and how you felt.

Tools for Journaling

For journaling, don't just stick to black pens and plain fonts. You can choose from numerous pens and colors to journal with and the variety of fonts you can use is wide ranging. (See Chapter 6 for more on the range of writing tools suitable for scrapbooking.)

Journaling templates are fun shapes with lines for journaling. You can also buy templates that have lines for straight, no-fail journaling.

If you like rubber stamps, there are stamps available that have designs with text lines for journaling. Stamp on your page, and you have an instant place to add your story. You can also use alphabet stamps to create clever journaling.

Oftentimes, you will want to draw attention to the words on the page. You can do so by using unique items to create words. Try using alphabet beads, metal charms with descriptive words printed on them, or bits and pieces from greeting cards.

The words speak for this page.

Layout with bead words.

I enjoy using sticker letters in unique ways to enhance the journaling in my scrapbook as well. When you have a long story to tell, take the opportunity to accent your story in a fun and meaningful way.

Some people ask if they should use their own handwriting for journaling or if they should use those cute computer fonts. This is a personal choice, and you can do some of both or go one way, but remember that your handwriting is precious to future generations.

Font collection is one of my newest hobbies. To get started check out these fabulous websites:

www.fontfree.com

www.fontgarden.com

www.wantedfonts.com

www.onescrappysite.com

www.ifree.com

A true friend. Note the use of different fonts.

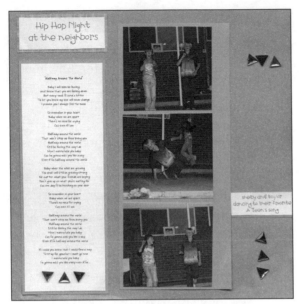

Font CD collections are a great place to start—very user friendly.

What to Say and Where to Find Inspiration for What to Say

Imagine running across a photo album of your ancestors from a hundred years ago. What would you like to know about your great, great, great, grandmother besides where the pictures were taken? I would want to know what her everyday life was like, what type of interests or hobbies she had. What was it like to live 100 years ago, what emotions did she experience?

What would you ask your ancestors? Now that you have this perspective think about what message you want to leave behind besides just the basics. Why do you love that which you photograph? Read on to learn how to get beyond the basics.

Beyond the Basics

You've answered the who, what, and why; now you want to include a little more detail in your scrapbook. Maybe you're working on pages for your son heading off to college or your daughter getting married. When you want to include more than just the basics of event journaling, where do you start?

Baby layout with a favorite lullaby.

Give your readers a backstage pass into your life by putting down in words the emotion behind the photo story. Below are some suggestions for getting beyond the basics in journaling.

Reverse Scrapbooking

I was first introduced to this method by Kim McCrary, a member of the editorial team of *Simple Scrapbooks* magazine, in a class she was teaching. Her suggestion was to think about a moment, feeling, or story that you want to express in your scrapbook and then go find a photo that does so. You are then starting backward, with the message first, then the photo.

For example, I wanted to explain to my children the importance of respecting the flag. I jotted down a few ideas for doing this and decided it would be best to do a scrapbook page demonstrating this respect. Through my photo search I found some photos from a family flag-raising ceremony with my children all watching as the flag was raised. From the photo you got a sense of reverence in the body language of those in the photo. I gathered these photos and then put them on a scrapbook page along with my written message.

Here are some ideas for reverse scrapbooking:

◆ **Traditions/holidays.** What traditions are important in your family and why? How did they get started? Why do you carry them on?

◆ **Namesake.** Why did you give your children (or pets) the names you did? Do you have photos of the person they are named after?

◆ **Why I love.** What is it you love about your partner, children, pets, hobbies?

Educate/Teach

Now you want to educate the viewer of the scrapbook on everything from how your children got their names to why you feel education in your family is so important. I have recently (along with many others) discovered the simplicity and ease of using quotes in my scrapbook. I can find quotes that not only convey the lesson I am trying to teach but convey it eloquently as well.

No matter how little money and how few possessions you own, having a dog makes you rich. – Louis Sabin

Layout with teaching type of quote on it.

Here are some favorite quote sites:

www.azlyrics.com
Search for song lyrics

www.personal.umich.edu/~pfa/ dreamhouse/nursery/rhymes
Nursery rhymes and more

www.twopeasinabucket.com/words.asp
Just for scrapbookers

creativequotations.com
Interesting categories

www.quotegarden.com
Includes occasion and sentiment listing such as sympathy to Earth Day

Connections

We are all connected in some way and it is fascinating to sit down and discover how. I wanted my children to feel connected to those ancestors who sacrificed to come and settle in America; telling them stories every Memorial Day just wasn't enough. So I made a scrapbook about their ancestors who are buried in a local city cemetery. I did this by going to the city cemetery where many of their relatives are buried and found out where they came from, their stories, and their sacrifices. I then compiled this information into a scrapbook to take with us every Memorial Day so my children can better understand their connection to these people.

A Heading Is Worth a Thousand Words

A heading is the title of your layout. It says a lot about your page and is a fun way to include journaling. I love to use fun headings on all of my pages. You can do so much with these!

Just as a headline is critical to a newspaper story, headings are a critical part of journaling because they can tie everything together and control the presentation and written aspect of the page. It's best to make headings short and sweet, easy to read, and eye-catching. For Justin's birthday pages, some of the headings I used were, "Presents, Presents, and More Presents," "Time to Celebrate," and "Digging Into My Cake."

Coming up with cute phrases and headings used to be a hard part of scrapbooking. Fortunately, there are now reference books with great scrapbook titles included, listed by category, as well as many websites with topper ideas. Pre-illustrated page titles are perfect for this. Some scrapbook magazines include titling ideas that you can copy into your scrapbook and color. (See Chapter 9 for pre-illustrated page title layout ideas.)

A Clean, Well-Lined Space for Writing

Now that you know what to write, you may be wondering where to write it. As you look through the following layouts, let your imagination wander as to where you can put your journaling to make your pages more interesting and meaningful.

◆ **Create a journaling block, by far the most tried and true method.** Compile your words onto a block of text that fits on your scrapbook page. You can mount the block of text onto another piece of paper to draw attention to the words if needed. Try adding a simple accent to the journaling block such as a small sticker or scrap of pattern paper.

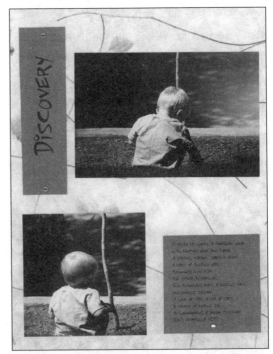

Journaling block. The block of text fits just perfectly into this layout, emphasizing the words while not overtaking the layout.

◆ **Tag, you're it!** A favorite discovery of scrapbookers is using the everyday tag previously used just for shipping or for noting prices. These tags can now be found in scrapbooks all over the country. We love to use these as the base for accents. The way a tag frames its attachments is charming. Another popular use for tags is journaling. Try writing directly on the tag, stamping on it, or adhering your computer-generated journaling. Regardless of what you do you will fall in love with using tags for your writing.

Circle tags dangling from photo. Here the words are included inside the middle of the circular tags to give the reader a feeling of connection.

◆ **Envelopes.** A fun way to bring focus to the words on the page is to use an envelope to enclose those sayings. Try inserting your journaling in a see-through envelope for a new journaling twist.

Layout using rectangular tags. The words are included on these rectangular tags, just the perfect size for this page.

Vellum envelope with journaling inside for a unique design twist.

The words appear to be almost floating on this layout, perfect for this father-daughter page.

Here, the words are printed in a bold font onto colored cardstock and then placed in a transparent envelope for a fun design twist.

◆ Using vellum paper in your journaling adds a different look to your scrapbook. Your words almost appear as if they are floating on top of the paper because the paper is translucent, not transparent. Try attaching the vellum with ribbon or eyelets for a perfect design flair.

◆ For a different look, try writing on a die cut. Use a die cut that matches the theme of your page, such as journaling on an apple die cut for a school page. Or trace a shape from a template and write inside it.

◆ Incorporate journaling into your page decorations by journaling around the border. Add some stickers here and there, and you've got a cute page.

◆ Be creative and use journaling as an accent, as well. Make a journaling puzzle that leads the reader through the story in a unique way.

From the Archives

Melody Ross, the creator of many journaling tools, was nicknamed Chatterbox as a child because she talked so much. That is now the name of her company. Look for Chatterbox products listing different heading suggestions and much more.

The Handwriting on the Wall

My mother does not like her handwriting, but the rest of us like it because it reminds us of our mother's love. To me, her handwriting evokes memories of handwritten school notes excusing me for being absent, recipes I read of hers when I was learning to cook, opening Christmas presents that always said, "From Mom and Dad" (but we knew that Mom picked them out), and the day's to-do list written by the phone, reminding her to wash laundry and drive us to the orthodontist's office.

Shortcuts

When tracing these templates, use a pencil and a soft eraser that you can use without damaging the paper.

Now my mother's handwriting means a carefully packed care package full of hand-sewn pajamas, discounted chocolates for me, crayons and markers for the kids, to-do lists detailing what tasks she wants to accomplish at my house, reminders for craft projects she wants to complete when she gets home, and a running grocery list for my house. I love my mother's handwriting because it reminds me of my mother's sacrifices and love for her children. So take this into consideration when trying to decide whether to include your own writing.

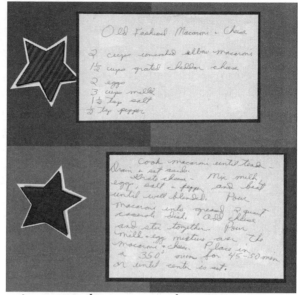

A way to always remember my mom—a favorite recipe handwritten.

Putting It All Together—Creating a Family History Scrapbook

Someone's heritage is something that is passed down from generation to generation like a legacy or inheritance. It can also be thought of as the traditions that get passed down in a family or community.

Answer these true/false questions to determine if you're a good candidate for writing a personal history:

I had a good childhood.

I had a bad childhood.

I am very young.

I am very old.

I received an extensive education.

I didn't go to school past the third grade.

I have several children.

I have no children.

I am close to my extended family.

I rarely speak to my relatives.

I am an excellent writer.

My writing is atrocious.

I had an eventful, colorful life.

My life was simple, filled with ordinary events.

If you answered true to any of these questions, you should write a personal history! Each person has a life worth recording, regardless of how ordinary it seems to you.

If you would rather, get a tape recorder and record your thoughts and memories on tape. Once you have recorded on tape, you can save the cassette in your scrapbook in one of the 3-D keepsake holders, or you can transcribe the words into text. If you are interested in creating a transcript of your interviews, you can do it yourself or pay a transcriber to do it for you.

Whether you write your memories or record them, the first place to start is with you. Let's say that the bare-bones facts you know about your family are as follows:

◆ Your father comes from a family that is of German and English Protestant background. Your paternal grandmother immigrated to the United States from Germany with her family in the 1920s. She came with her mother and great-aunt, and they settled in New York City.

◆ Your paternal grandfather's family had been in this country for a long time and were of English descent. He died when your father was 10, and you don't know much about him except that he was a commercial artist.

◆ Your mother comes from a Russian Jewish family. Your maternal grandmother's family immigrated to the United States from Russia at the turn of the century and also settled in New York. Her father (your great-grandfather) was a rabbi.

◆ You don't know anything about your maternal grandfather.

These explorations might leave you very curious. You might be interested in finding out what area of Germany your grandmother came from and exactly where they settled in New York. Both sides of this family likely came through Ellis Island in New York City—what was this like? Where in Russia did your mother's family come from? The religious background of this family might interest you—what was the rabbi grandfather's life like in the old country? You might want information on your maternal grandfather. And where did your paternal grandfather learn his trade as a commercial artist? What kinds of places did he work for?

Think about where you could go to fill in whatever information you are interested in finding out.

From the Archives

From 1892 to 1954, Ellis Island in New York City was the entry point for 12 million immigrants to the United States. Today, more than 40 percent of Americans, 100 million people, can trace their roots to an Ellis Island ancestor. At the Ellis Island Immigration Museum and Immigration History Center, people can find information about their families. You can even honor an immigrant relative by having his or her name put up on the Ellis Island Wall of Honor.

Some of us come from families that have been in a certain community for many generations, others are from families whose ancestors came to this country during the great immigrant waves in the early 1900s, and others came from recently immigrated families that have been in the United States for only a generation or two. Your focus will depend on your access to resources, and your interests. If you don't have any historical information farther back than two generations, then focus on two generations and include what you know of the previous ones. If you wish to go back farther and have the resources, do it.

See if you can interview family members. This can be a great job for the kids. Sometimes older people are more willing to talk to children than to adults. If you'd like to make a history of your parents, sic one of your kids on them! Arm her with a few loaded questions, a tape recorder, and that irresistible grin, and you'll get all sorts of unexpected revelations.

Here is a list of questions your kids can ask to get the conversation rolling:

- ◆ What kind of pets did you have in your house?
- ◆ Did you get along with your siblings when you were growing up?
- ◆ What church (if any) did you belong to as a child?
- ◆ Tell me your favorite activity when you were growing up.

- ◆ Did you get in trouble when you were young? What for?
- ◆ What things did you do on your birthday?
- ◆ Tell me about the first time you met Grandpa/Grandma.
- ◆ What was it like when you drove a car for the first time?
- ◆ What were your favorite holiday traditions growing up?

When gathering family history, don't forget other family fixtures: your next-door neighbor, the lady who used to baby-sit you after school, or the man your family rented a cabin from every summer. They can give you a different perspective on events and people.

From the Archives

A book by Don Norton, *Composing Your Life Story*, includes 500 topics for making a personal history. These topics include vocational choices, favorite family stories, favorite places, leisure activities, family shopping, naps, childhood friends, hairstyles, typical weekday routines, higher education, family recipes, and nicknames to cite a few. Choose a topic that is interesting to you and write what you can about it.

Remember to have fun with your journaling!

As you are gathering this information, you need to have a place to store everything. I suggest purchasing a good-size plastic file box that enables you to hang file folders and store documents and photographs. Organize the files to coordinate with your timeline and store documentation and photographs in separate folders in the same slot.

Now you have information on your family, you're organized, and you know where you are going. What's next? You start putting all this great material in a scrapbook.

You'll want to get your usual basic tools together:

♦ An album
♦ Paper—cardstock and decorative
♦ Tools for journaling
♦ Scissors
♦ Page protectors (recommended for use in this book, especially if some of the items included are fragile)
♦ Adhesives
♦ Embellishments you think you might want to use
♦ pH testing pen and deacidification spray

You'll want to choose an album and materials that complement your subject matter, and for this one, it's a good idea to keep the embellishments simple and tasteful. I suggest using classic colors and classic embellishments, such as photo corners. Many embellishment manufacturers have a selection of appropriate products for this. Take a look at some idea books to see how other people with the same type of project have designed their books. Remember, for this project, you want to focus on the history and writing, not the punch art.

Because this is a scrapbook meant to last, choosing archival-quality materials is of the utmost importance. You don't want to gather all these precious items, only to have them deteriorate. Be careful when handling them and be sure to deacidify any items, such as newspaper clippings, which might fall apart.

As you work on the book, make sure to include a lot of journaling that describes not only what is happening in the pictures you include, but also information about historical events during the time when the photo was taken, stories you heard about the people pictured, family legends, quotes and poems by writers of each era you cover, song lyrics that recall the times, and more.

When this book is completed, it will be a lasting, much-cherished tribute to your family—and will tell a story not only of the people in the family, but of the times they lived in. And for you, it will help you learn much more about people you know and the community you live in. And, by the way, it will help you hone your scrapbooking skills to a sharp edge.

The Least You Need to Know

◆ Remember to include the who, what, where, when, and why when journaling the story.

◆ Include all the funny stories about pictures. These will have you holding your sides for years to come.

◆ There are some fun journaling tools to help you create great pages.

◆ Even if you don't like your handwriting, be sure to include some of it in your scrapbook.

◆ If you are interested in working on a scrapbook that documents your family's history, look in this chapter for ideas and a step-by-step guide.

In This Chapter

◆ Making the most of storage in your home and on the go

◆ Minimize frustration by organizing your supplies

◆ Making scrapbooking feasible so you aren't scrambling to find your supplies to sneak in some time

◆ Less really is more

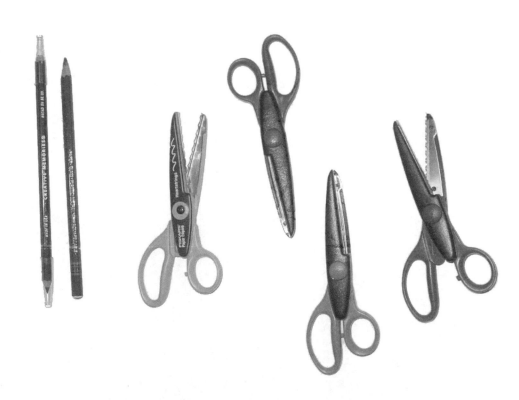

Chapter 13

Create a Fun and Inviting Workspace

Does this sound familiar: It's Saturday morning, and you have a few spare hours. Perfect time to scrapbook, right? So you drag your box of photos upstairs and place them on the kitchen table. You head back downstairs for your box of paper and notice the pile of dirty clothes outside the laundry room. After throwing the clothes in the washer, you head back upstairs, but halfway up, you remember your box and turn around to get it. After 15 minutes of choosing photos for your layout, the phone rings. It's Aunt Ettie, reminding you to bring a potato salad to the church picnic. After disentangling yourself from her, you sit down again. You work for five solid minutes when you notice that your time is up, and you need to put everything away. Frustrated, you think, "Scrapbooking is so time-consuming!"

Some people prefer to do their scrapbooking at home and have plenty of space, others prefer to work on the go, and still others cram in their scrapping wherever they can. Whichever kind of scrapper you are, you'll need to organize your supplies, create a good and inviting workspace, store your materials, and, most of all, make the time for an activity you enjoy.

Less Is More

Organizing your scrapbook supplies begins before you go to the scrapbook store. Remember, you don't want to buy things you don't need or duplicates of things you already have.

You know how they say you shouldn't go grocery shopping when you're hungry or without a list because you're likely to end up buying much more than you need? The same goes for buying scrapping supplies. A while ago, I went to my favorite scrapbook store to see what

I could see. I found some great birthday stickers. "These will be perfect for Justin's birthday page," I told myself. "I'll buy two sets just to be sure I have enough." A few weeks later, as I was setting up my supplies, I found three more. After you have your supplies, the next step is to find good ways to organize them. To determine what your storage needs are, answer the following questions:

1. You do most of your scrapbooking:

   a. At home in a specially designated scrapbooking room.

   b. At workshops, crops, or with a scrapbooking group.

   c. Anywhere from your next door neighbor's house to your kitchen table.

2. Which of the following describes your current storage situation?

   a. I live in a huge house and have unlimited space.

   b. I do all my scrapping outside my house so I need portable storage.

   c. All my supplies are crammed under my bed, on top of the fridge, and on the top shelf of my closet.

3. When selecting storage supplies:

   a. I want to use items I already have on hand.

   b. I use something that's easy to transport.

   c. I'm more concerned with being able to locate supplies than purchasing the latest gadgets.

4. What are your shopping habits?

   a. I'm a sucker for gadgets and tools that make scrapbooking easier.

   b. I don't purchase many tools because I use the ones at the store.

   c. I buy the products I like and know I'll use.

Add up your score using the following scorecard:

A = 3 points

B = 5 points

C = 7 points

What range do you fall into?

12 to 15 points = Home office scrapper

16 to 21 points = On-the-go scrapper

22 to 28 points = Kitchen-table scrapper

Using these categories as a guide, read the corresponding advice on setting up your own scrapbooking space. Each section includes advice for your particular needs, but remember to be flexible and creative. The last section contains tips on storing favorite products.

The Home Office Scrapper—the Den at Your Disposal

Even if you have plenty of space for your scrapbook supplies, you may have a hard time keeping things organized. For example, do you wander into your scrapbook room and find it hard to remember where you put those back-to-school stickers or the embossed vellum paper for your wedding album? Well, read on for a description of an easy-to-use scrapbooking room for the *home office scrapper*.

Words for Posterity _____

Home office scrapper—this lucky individual has an entire room in which to work on scrapbooks. Although this is an ideal situation, be careful to keep supplies organized.

Workspace

The first item you'll need in the home office is a desk, preferably one with drawers of various sizes. If you don't have a desk, a table with a file cabinet and some storage containers would make a good substitute. Use the small drawers for things like pens and adhesives and place large supplies in the file drawers—templates, idea books, class handouts, and things like this work well here.

Storage

I like to store my cardstock upright in a filing container so I can see the colors rather than storing it flat on shelves.

Another way to organize your paper is to purchase two large accordion-style folders, which are sold at office supply stores. Use one to store paper sorted by color and the other to store paper sorted by theme.

You'll want to put your templates in folders in the file drawers, arranged by category in alphabetical order. When placing several templates in one folder, place a sheet of paper between the individual templates to keep them from getting tangled up. If you've got a large number of templates, it's a good idea to keep a numbered list of them, with a corresponding list on each template. This helps you when you can't remember if you filed your soccer templates under _F_ for fall or _S_ for sports. For

example, if the soccer puzzle mate is number 12 in your system, place that on your master list—having a master list makes things much easier to find.

Sticky Points _____

Remember to look through your scraps before you cut up a new piece of paper. You can get a lot of mileage out of your scraps by using them for punches and other small accents.

The next necessary item is a bookcase or shelving system on which you can place binders filled with stickers, die cuts, and other small items, as well as your scrapbooks in progress. Boxes of sheet protectors can go on the shelves, too.

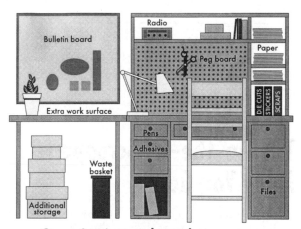

**Organization and good storage—
a perfect workspace.**

Create a nice ambiance in your office—it's as important as having the proper storage space and efficient files. Choose lighting in your space that provides both good overhead light for when you're looking through your supply bins and good bright spot lighting for when you're working up close with pictures and other items in your scrapbook. A good idea is to buy an inexpensive desk lamp to go over your work area—generally incandescent light is easier on the eyes than fluorescent light and provides bright, natural light. Try burning a scented candle to add to the atmosphere and help you relax. What a difference this makes! Also, why not bring a radio into your room so that you can enjoy listening to your favorite CDs or radio station if you're scrapbooking by yourself? This room is where your creativity comes alive, so make it as cozy and comfortable as you like.

Shortcuts

Do you have a friend who likes scrapbooking too? Try this: Each of you get subscriptions to different scrapbooking magazines and trade with each other. You'll be up-to-date on all the latest in scrapbooking without spending a ton of money.

The best way to stay organized when you have a home office is to take inventory frequently and put everything away when you're done. Good luck!

The On-the-Go Scrapper— Away You Go!

If you're an *on-the-go scrapper*, you first need to determine where you're going to store your scrapbook items in between crops and workshops. Even if you have only a small amount of space, you can store many things if you use the right products.

You basically have two options—purchase a storage item made just for scrapbooking products or use storage products that you can purchase at mass-merchant stores.

From the Archives

The consumer drives the scrapbooking market and demands products. In this category it is especially true as scrapbookers know what items they need to store. One successful company, Crop In Style, was created by a husband and wife team and has remained at the forefront in setting industry trends.

There is a scrapbook tote to meet everyone's needs—from super deluxe to simple storage. To determine what will fit your needs you first need to map out what you want the item to tote. Do you want it to contain all of your supplies? Or just your nonconsumable supplies, such as punches, pens, or cutters? Will you take this with you on the road or keep it at home? I find that a tote works well for storing all those nonconsumable products and to store your current projects.

Kitchen-Table Scrapper— Wherever and Whenever

If you don't have much room to store your supplies, you need to be creative to think of new spaces. I had friends who lived in a two-bedroom apartment with three kids and used every available inch of space for storage, including raising their bed up with cinder blocks so they could use the space underneath. Look around your house: Is there room under your bed or in the linen closet? What about building some shelves in your bedroom to store your supplies? Just remember to keep in mind these storage rules: Avoid moisture, temperature fluctuation, and humidity. Try not to use the basement, attic, or garage for your supplies. Also, make sure you have put supplies where you can get to them easily.

Be creative when coming up with storage options. The most important thing is to keep things organized and readily available. I advise the *kitchen-table scrapper* to organize scrapping at home in a two-part process. First, spend some time grouping pictures together and deciding what you want to do with them, maybe sketching out layout ideas or creating a folder with your pictures and the supplies needed to create the page or pages. When you shop to get supplies, put them directly into the folder and store this in a file bin. Then, when you have your other supplies organized and stored on one shelf of a closet or bookcase, you will be ready to scrap at a moment's notice.

Words for Posterity

The **kitchen-table scrapper** fits supplies wherever they can possibly go: in the closet, behind the sofa, or even in kitchen cabinets—wherever supplies are easy to grab and use. You'll find her scrapbooking at the kitchen table or on a card table in the family room.

Extra Storage Ideas for the Avid Scrapper

If you are an avid scrapbooker like myself and you have been collecting supplies for a while, you may find you have as much or more than a small store. You need extra storage savvy—here are some ideas.

Bind It Up

Binders are so versatile, so easy to use, and so compact that you'll find they can fill many of your storage needs. For instance, you can buy binders especially designed to hold stickers, which have refillable pages that have different-sized pockets. The binder measures 12 × 12 and features a wrap-around zipper so your stickers cannot fall out. Or you can try the binders made to hold baseball cards. Use the different protectors with photo sleeve pockets for larger stickers. If you are ambitious, you can even make sticker storage sheets from page protectors. Simply sew some pockets of varying sizes onto the protector with your sewing machine, using a heavy-duty needle.

Templates are perfect to store in binders; just place a sheet of paper in between each one so they don't get tangled. Organize these by category, and you're set. If you have large templates, try punching a hole in a corner of each one and storing them on a metal ring. I also like to store a pencil, sharpener, and wax pencil with my templates so I don't have to look everywhere when it is time to trace.

Shortcuts

Make sure you label your binders on the spine so you can easily see what is in them.

Die cuts work well in binders, too. You probably went to a lot of trouble to make those die cuts, so make sure you store them in such a way that they won't rip or bend. You can use binders for storing your photo corners, punches, and scraps. I like to organize these by category, such as holidays, dances, or birthdays. This way, you can flip to find the supplies you need without any hassle.

Storing Paper

You've got to have paper on hand when you want to scrapbook, but how do you store it without creasing it? Some of my students use expandable folders, but that doesn't work well for me because my paper always gets crumpled. I like to use a plastic file box because it is sturdy enough to protect my paper but lightweight enough for me to haul around with ease. I store it lengthwise, so I can see at a glance what colors and patterns I have to work with. If you must store your paper on a shelf, try not to stack it more than three inches high, or it will have a tendency to slip and fall.

If you don't have large amounts of paper to store, use an oversize sheet protector and organize your paper by color. Place the protectors in a binder, and you've got all your paper at your fingertips! This works well for paper packs, too.

Paper that is size 12 × 12 inches is difficult to store because there aren't many ready-made commercial products that come in that size. You either have to buy products made for 12 × 12 scrapbooking or improvise. Some of the best storage options I have seen are oversized storage containers with a lid—paper is placed on its side and other supplies are next to it. Also, for those who have lots of 12 × 12 paper, try using your cleaned-out pizza boxes to store your paper in for temporary purposes. This can be successful and is a good way to recycle those boxes.

Shortcuts

If you go to crops or scrapbooking parties and bring your supplies with you, mark your initials on them with a permanent pen to avoid losing them.

Sticky Points

Remember, you don't need to bring every pen you own to crops and workshops. When other participants see your collection, they'll want to borrow them. That's fine, but these pens can be misused—too much pressure will ruin many pen tips. Try bringing only the essential pens to class—remember that you can always journal at home.

Storing Punches

If you are a punch fan, you ought to buy a tackle box (or if someone you know goes fishing, "borrow" theirs). Clear plastic makeup storage boxes with lots of little drawers are good, too. Another favorite for punches are the boxes designed for storing embroidery floss. This is a great way to store your punches and be able to see what you've got. You don't want to buy a punch on sale, only to find that you've got one just like it at home.

Wherever and whenever you do your scrapbooking, it's a time for you to get creative and enjoy doing your own thing. If you meet with people to work on your scrapbooks, remember that the point is not to compete with the others but to share ideas and get inspired by the creativity of your fellow scrappers. Relax and enjoy the camaraderie. If you work at home, in whatever space you use, organization can be the key to making scrapbooking possible and making a little space for yourself in the midst of your busy life. Do it before the children are awake or when they are out with friends. Turn on the phone answering machine, turn up the Mozart, and have fun!

The Least You Need to Know

- ◆ It's best to take note of supplies you need before you go shopping.
- ◆ Organization of your supplies and space is key to enjoying scrapbooking.
- ◆ Where do you scrapbook? In a home office? On the go? Or anywhere you can find space? This can determine what sort of storage is best for you.
- ◆ Scrapbooking is a wonderful, creative outlet—make sure your space is comfortable, and your time is your own. Enjoy it!

In This Part

Part 4

Scrap It, Stick It, Store It

You own the supplies and you've attended the classes, yet you still struggle when it comes to creating satisfying scrapbook pages. You're not alone. Many scrapbookers, long confident in their knowledge and use of tools, still struggle with design. As you read these design guidelines, think of your own pages and you'll be surprised at how many rules come naturally to you. In this part, you'll get advice on making the best color choices for your scrapbook, places to build your own scrapbook community to keep you motivated, and style suggestions that fit your personality.

In This Chapter

◆ What is a "community"?

◆ How attending classes at your local scrapbook store can keep you motivated

◆ Discovering an online community that suits your needs

◆ What you should bring to a consumer convention

Chapter **14**

Building Your Own Scrapbooking Community

Connecting with people interested in the same hobbies as you is fulfilling. You can build new friendships, share ideas, and provide motivation to your fellow scrapbookers. Finding a place to meet other scrapbookers is what this chapter is all about. Whether it's at your local scrapbook store or an online message board, you'll learn about different scrapbooking communities, what these communities can do for you, and how to access them.

The Strangest Places

A scrapbooking community should have these four qualities to truly work and keep you coming back:

◆ **Education.** With the constant influx of new scrapbooking products and techniques, it's difficult to stay on top of things. Your community can help its members explore these and decide what best meets their needs and educate them. Education could take the form of an instructional class, online posting of layouts showing new products being used, or a vendor "make it and take it" mini class.

◆ **Support.** Scrapbookers need to share their enthusiasm with others who appreciate it. My husband can only say the word cute so many times in a day. (I was showing him some new stickers I had gotten and he just couldn't manage to say cute one more time.) As scrapbookers, we love to talk about our hobby and everything related to it—from scrapbook celebrity sightings to the latest technique craze. You can find this support on message boards, at crops, and through magazine articles.

◆ **Inspiration.** Many of us love to read and hear about other people's lives; it's why we read those celebrity magazines or watch those stories on *Oprah*. We can be inspired in many ways and one of them is to hear about others' triumphs. A triumph may be as simple as completing a Fiftieth Wedding Anniversary album or winning a page layout contest. Hearing these stories inspires us and reminds us why we create scrapbooks. So look to your community to inspire you with success stories, personal triumphs, or …

◆ **Motivation.** Now that you are educated, supported, and inspired, you need one more thing: motivation. Your community can help you with this in a variety of ways. My all-time favorite method of motivation is the "Scrappers Challenge" Yahoo mailing group led by Rockster (her online name). This is a website totally dedicated to keeping you on top of your scrapbooking, from organization to completion of a certain number of pages per time period. I have seen stores and websites that have monthly challenges from total pages to a specific topic to tackle. This is where it will all come together.

Sticky Points

I often meet people who spend much of their time posting on Internet boards, looking at magazines and idea books, or participating in swaps—and who rarely complete a scrapbook page. While there is nothing wrong with relying on your community connections, remember to use them to support and encourage your work, not distract you from it.

Scrapbook Magazines

I love getting my scrapbook magazines in the mail. I can always find a new idea or use for a product, interesting layouts, and motivating tips. I enjoy quickly glancing through the magazine, then, when I have more time, going through it cover to cover. Then I go back and rip out my favorite layouts and file them for future inspiration. I enjoy being educated about new techniques and products and love the ideas for new projects. Try not to get overwhelmed when you see some of the complex layouts, just enjoy. It's fun to duplicate layouts and add your own flair.

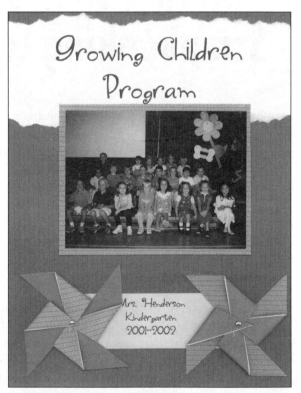

Layout showing windmills as accents. This is a technique I learned about from a magazine, one of my favorite ways to stay on top of all the trends. Not only did I have fun making this accent, but my kids wanted to do their own.

A layout I cased.

Here is a quick reference to the top current scrapbooking magazines and their websites (if they have them):

Creating Keepsakes
www.creatingkeepsakes.com

Memory Makers
www.memorymakersmagazine.com

Ivy Cottage Creations
www.ivycottagecreations.com

PaperKuts
www.paperkuts.com

Simple Scrapbooks
www.simplescrapbooksmag.com

Scrapbooks, ETC.

You can pick all of these up your local scrapbook store, Wal-Mart, or craft store. Check out their websites for archived articles. If you're interested in purchasing back issues, go to eBay—you will often find scrapbookers selling their wares. To find out what your average consumer thinks of a publication, you can read reviews at www.scrapbookaddict.com (go to the "mag talk" link).

Here are my three favorite "flipping" tips:

◆ As you flip through your new magazine, mark your favorite layouts so you'll be able to find them later.

◆ Take note of the ads. Advertisements often include innovative ways to use their new products.

◆ Look at the graphic design of the magazine itself to see how its editors and designers use borders, pattern paper, and scissors.

Words for Posterity

CASE is an online acronym meaning Copy And Steal Everything. If you CASE a layout, you duplicate the page or project.

Your Local Scrapbook Store

We all love to shop, don't we? What better way to connect to your fellow scrapbookers than by participating in activities at your local scrapbook store (hopefully you have one nearby)? You can enjoy your store in other ways than just shopping (though that is my personal favorite)—you can take classes, attend workshops, and receive personalized shopping advice.

Attending classes and workshops is not only good for getting those pages done, but for sharing your hobby with others who appreciate it. How many of us have excitedly shown a prized layout to someone "out of the loop" only to hear something like "Neat pictures"? When you show the same prized layout to a fellow scrapbooker they immediately give you the praises you deserve for the effort and brilliance behind the page. I enjoy getting together with other scrappers and just talking about favorite products, scrapbook celebrities, and more. I am always motivated by the stories I hear from these women I meet as well. I leave the class more determined than ever to continue participating in this pastime.

Layout using a "shaker box" technique I learned at a class. This technique isn't difficult but does take a little bit of time and practice.

> **Words for Posterity** _____
>
> A **shaker box** is a 3-D accent made by creating two hollow square frames and gluing them on top of each other with decorative accents in the middle that move when you shake the page.

> **Shortcuts** _____
>
> Give your feedback and comments to the store personnel. They may be influenced by your suggestions and buy that new product line that you told them about.

These scrapbook stores have websites that post pictures of their stores, schedules of their classes, and the newest products:

> www.archiversonline.com
>
> www.victoriaskeepsakes.com
>
> www.scrappys.net
>
> www.creativeyou.com
>
> www.scrapbooksensations.com

To find a store near you, look in the back of your scrapbooking magazines or go to the store locater at the following websites:

> www.creatingkeepsakes.com
>
> www.memorymakersmagazine.com

Online Community

Access online communities and you will find articles illustrating new techniques, layouts showing the newest products available, and of course friends to chat with. Another enjoyable aspect of the web is viewing and posting layouts on the websites. You can upload your layouts to show your fellow scrappers what you're working on and share your own tips. Most websites also have some sort of design team, a group of very talented scrapbookers, who will post layouts according to a pre-determined theme. This is very inspiring as you see the latest products and techniques in action. The people involved in these communities are very cutting edge and can really give your scrapbooking a boost.

I learned about paper tearing and rolling through a post on a scrapbook board. To achieve this look, tear your paper and then slightly wet the torn edge. You can then roll the paper into the direction you want.

Try these online communities for the best of the best on the web:

> www.scrapbooking.com
>
> www.scrapjazz.com
>
> www.gracefulbee.com
>
> www.twopeasinabucket.com
>
> www.scrapbookaddict.com

Remember to be careful about giving out your personal information when online. You can create a profile for yourself—but don't get too personal.

Swaps

Suppose you want to buy the latest color of eyelets, but you know you won't use the entire package of 100. What do you do? You could participate in an eyelet swap.

Swaps—a "swap meet" of sorts in which a group of scrappers exchange scrapbooking materials through a hostess, expanding their personal inventories and saving themselves some time and money—are taking the scrapbooking world by storm. There are three varieties of swaps: the product swap, the completed project swap, and the surprise swap.

Product Swap

A product swap is where a group of scrappers purchase a pre-determined amount and type of a particular product—for example, eyelets. Everyone then sends the product to the swap hostess. After she has received all submissions, she divides them up equally and sends them back to the participants. I once participated in a printed vellum swap. I purchased 24 of one unique vellum pattern and swapped them with 11 other scrappers. I received back 11 different patterns of vellum (2 of each). Thus, I was able to expand my selection of vellum without killing my wallet.

A different flavor of product swap is when one ambitious person will hostess a swap where you send money and the hostess buys a large quantity of the product you have signed up to swap. The hostess then divides the product up and mails it to you. This works well when you only want a small amount of a certain product. I recently did this with poetry dog tags, which are available online at the rate of $20.00 for 250. The swap cost $4.50 (including shipping) and I received forty of the tags. These types of swaps are my favorite to participate in.

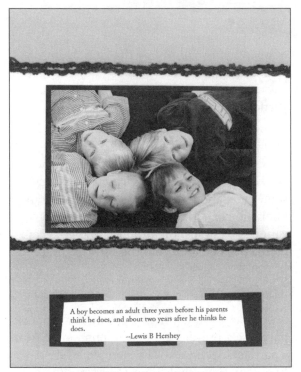

Fibers from a product swap.

Layout using USA tags from my sister Laurie's swap.

Completed Project Swap

A completed project swap is where your options include only completed projects—anything from paper piecing to shaker boxes. Completed project swaps are usually organized around a theme, such as winter, birthdays, and so on. The hostess dictates the rules for the completed projects, such as the number of accents required. Before trying this type of swap, I suggest that you try to check out items that participating scrappers have done previously so you won't be disappointed. Oftentimes, you can view the participating swappers' previous items online posted by themselves or others. This will give you an idea of whether it's the type of style you're looking for.

Surprise Swap

You can count on being surprised in these swaps! There are a variety of ways to participate in a surprise swap and you will find different versions posted everywhere on the web. For example, you can sign up to be a secret pal. You receive and send scrapbook goodies in an established time frame. If you love to get mail and be surprised, then a surprise swap is perfect for you.

Here is a tried-and-true swap board with a moderator to help keep everybody in line:

mb.twopeasinabucket.com/
postlist.php?Cat=&Board=UBB3

Here is another one I am trying out:

www.scrapjazz.com/community/jazzclub/
forumdisplay.php?s=&forumid=13

Conventions

Envision thousands of scrapbookers roaming the aisles of a massive convention hall loaded with scrapbook supplies. Yes, it is a sight to see! A convention is a great place to purchase your supplies, because often the attending manufacturers will sell direct—you are sure to get a price break on the last day. You will find classes and *make-it-and-take-its* everywhere you look. These consumer conventions have been so successful that you can probably find one near home no matter where you live. They usually last a couple of days and offer a variety of activities. You can meet your favorite scrapbook celebrity, attend an all-night crop, or see the latest products available. So gather up your friends and plan a get-away that will get your creative juices flowing for months to come.

> ### Words for Posterity
>
> A **make-it-and-take-it** is a project that you do right there. For example, you walk the convention floor and stop at your favorite manufacturer's booth, where they're making shaker boxes. You get to sit down at the project table, have all the supplies handed to you, and complete the project right there.

If you have a favorite manufacturer, oftentimes they will have a link on their website to conventions they will be attending such as this popular manufacturer:

www.makingmemories.com

You can also go to these favorite convention sites for info on upcoming conventions:

www.memoryexpo.com

www.becreativeexpo.com

Participating in vendor demonstrations encourages you to try new products, as in this layout.

Here are some tips to get the most out of attending a convention:

- **Travel light.** You will want to bring all your newfound goodies home. Scrapbookers have been known to have to ship stuff UPS from the convention center because of all the shopping they did.
- **Map it out.** If possible get a list of attending companies and highlight the ones you just have to see. It's easy to get distracted and not make it to all the booths.
- **Get smart.** The classes at these conventions are top notch. Many are taught by the manufacturers and you are sure to get instructed on the latest techniques.

◆ **Be prepared.** Wear comfortable walking shoes and bring a bag with wheels so you don't have to carry everything on your shoulder.

◆ **Be a savvy shopper.** Remember that those exhibiting had to bring all of their wares with them and will typically offer a discount on the last day. If there is a hot item, though, make sure you pick it up when you find it because vendors do sell out.

Your Own Personal Consultant

I have always thought it would be great to have a personal secretary, someone to help you keep track of your life. Well you can have this in a small way if you choose to purchase supplies from a scrapbook consultant. There are some companies that sell only through their consultant base. One of the benefits is that the consultant hand delivers all of your purchases directly to your home. They will also invite you to classes and crops. You will be able to meet people in your area who are participating in this activity as well.

The downside is that you typically can only purchase one line from that consultant and you will find yourself paying a little bit of a higher price. If you run out of an item and your consultant isn't available, then you can't just run to the store and pick that item up. I recently attended a scrapbook party at a friend's home and found that the variety of products available was very limited.

Layout using product and ideas bought from CADD consultant.

Sticky Points

Remember that these consultants are out to make money and create friends so be honest and open about whether or not you plan to give them your business. It will save both of you time.

Shortcuts

To find consultants quickly, go to the website of the company you're interested in.

The following companies work with consultants:

www.creativememories.com

www.closetomyheart.com

www.stampinup.com

www.scrapinasnap.com

www.cockadoodledesign.com

I like to be involved in all of these forms of community and each one adds a different flavor to my scrapbooking. Find a community that best suits your needs; your scrapbooking will be enriched.

The Least You Need to Know

◆ A good scrapbooking community will educate, support, inspire, and motivate.

◆ If you plan to attend a convention, prepare ahead with a shopping list, good walking shoes, and lots of extra storage.

◆ Check your favorite website for the newest techniques and products.

In This Chapter

◆ Learn how to define your scrapbooking style

◆ How to make your scrapbook showcase your style

◆ Making time for scrapbooking in your busy life

◆ Streamline shopping by defining your supply needs

Chapter 15

Define Your Style, Determine Your Needs

If you're like most of the first-time students who take my basic scrapbooking classes, you are overwhelmed by all the different layouts and products you see. The most common question beginners ask is, "Can you give me some ideas on what to do with all these pictures?" My answer is absolutely, positively, *yes!*

Vive La Difference! There Is No "Right" Style

It's important to take a little time before you begin scrapbooking to discover your style. When I teach a scrapbook class, I invariably hear people say they are intimidated by the layouts they see in magazines. Those professional layouts can seem so difficult that people would rather give up than try to do something that elaborate. Participants sometimes come to a six-hour workshop, choose a store layout idea they like, and spend the entire time painstakingly replicating the layout with their own pictures.

The real secret is that there is no one correct way to scrapbook, no one perfect pen, no one must-have product. The only "right way" is the method that you prefer—the one that gets you to your goal. In this chapter, I will help you define your style and clarify your direction as a scrapper. Once you get that taken care of, the fun begins!

Sticky Points

Although it's fun to look at your friends' and neighbors' scrapbooks, try not to get caught up in comparing your skills. What matters most is that your personality comes through. Remember, you are creating a unique scrapbook; let yourself shine through.

Although you need to follow some basic design principles, there is no right style for a scrapbook because we all have different tastes.

Finding Your Style

Take a little time to flip through this book and mark the layouts you like with a paper clip or Post-it note. Do the same with layouts you dislike. Next, look at some scrapbooking magazines and *idea books* and tear out the layouts you like and dislike.

Words for Posterity

Don't know the difference between a scrapbooking magazine and an **idea book?** Although they look similar, there is a difference. Idea books are larger and often focus on specific events, such as weddings or vacations. They have fewer ads than magazines and fewer articles. Magazines, on the other hand, are published regularly and have regular articles. It's a good idea to subscribe to a magazine and purchase idea books that suit your needs.

The major scrapbooking magazines are *Creating Keepsakes, Memory Makers, Paper Kuts,* and *Simple Scrapbooks.* You can find most of them at your local craft stores, but some of the smaller ones are more difficult to locate. Many of them can be found in the major bookstore chains. Looking through magazines can really motivate you to work on your albums. Besides that, these magazines help keep track of all the newest scrapbooking products. Browse through several to see which ones you prefer and don't overlook the other craft magazines while you're there. Check out the stamping books for the latest techniques in that arena. You can look at *tole painting* magazines to see the most recent designs (such as sunflowers or frogs). Make sure you look at the interior design magazines for the latest color trends. You can even find inspiration in sewing magazines!

Words for Posterity

Tole painting is painting on wood using patterns that you can transfer onto the wood, typically done in a rustic style and depicting country scenes.

Now that you're familiar with available resources, you can decide which ones you'd like to buy and create a *favorites file* you can refer to. Now you are ready for the next step.

Words for Posterity

A **favorites file** is a personal book of ideas and layouts that you compile. Organize the files in a three-ring binder, file folder, manila envelope, or whatever is easiest (there's no need to buy archival materials for this).

Now that you have a favorites file look through the layouts you have selected and search for the commonalities. Is there a particular product you like more than others? Is there a color palette that you like more than others? Determining what visually appeals to you is key to determining your style. Go through the following list and check the items and the colors that were being used. Make notes to record other items you find in common.

Paper Colors
___ Primary
___ Bright/neon
___ Classic
___ Muted
___ Pastel

Paper Patterns
___ Specific
___ General
___ Black felt-tip
___ Colorful gel rollers
___ Paint pens
___ Coloring pencils
___ Colorful felt-tip

Decorative Tools
___ Scissors
___ Punches
___ Stamps
___ Shape cutter
___ Crimper

Stationery
___ Full sheet
___ Varying card size
___ Punch-outs

Page Toppers
___ Pre-cut shapes
___ Die cuts
___ Handmade scraps
___ Stickers
___ Letter shapes
___ Frames

Decorative Paper
___ Vellum
___ Corrugated
___ Metallic
___ Specialty packs
___ Handmade
___ Embossed
___ Pressed flower

From the Archives

Preserved, pressed flowers have been used as decorative accents through the ages. Old journals have been found with imprints of flowers smattering pages describing different aspects of everyday life. They depicted femininity and love of nature. These accents are now a favorite among scrapbookers and can be found at your local craft stores or scrapbook specialty stores.

Templates
___ Basic shapes
___ Elaborate shapes
___ Alphabet
___ Border Buddies
___ Journaling Genies
___ Puzzle mates

Mixed Media

___ Ribbon/trim

___ Eyelets/fasteners

___ Metal accents

___ Tags

___ Buttons

___ Beads

___ Wire

Miscellaneous _____

_____

_____

Make note of these items. If all your favorites include stickers, then spend some time at the sticker rack next time you go shopping. If it's the lettering that catches your eye, you might want to purchase a lettering book or take a class. Whatever it is, you'll want to repeat it in your own book.

Once you've gotten a feel for what you like, you are ready to move on to the next step.

Name That Style!

To further determine your style, take this fun quiz. Choose the answer to each question that best matches your personality. Remember that no one is looking, so be honest.

1. Your wardrobe consists of …

   a. Classic items—you want to dress like Lauren Bacall.

   b. Up-to-the-minute styles out of fashion magazines.

   c. Laura Ashley jumpers.

   d. Functional, sturdy clothes.

   e. Bright colors and lots of accessories.

   f. Whatever is clean and comfortable.

2. Your favorite activity is …

   a. Dinner and a movie.

   b. A trip to New York for a Broadway musical.

   c. Ordering pizza and watching the latest video release.

   d. Hiking and camping outdoors.

   e. Riding roller coasters, bungee jumping, anything adventurous.

   f. A writing workshop at the community college.

3. Your bedroom is decorated with …

   a. Muted natural colors and fabrics.

   b. Coordinating comforter, pillows, and curtains.

   c. Floral pillows, cute knickknacks, and handmade crafts.

   d. An antique dresser and a quilt your grandparents passed down.

   e. Brightly colored curtains, funky pillows, and patterned lampshades.

   f. Framed prints and a nightstand covered with books and papers.

4. Your makeup bag is …

   a. Neat and contains the bare essentials: lipstick, foundation, mascara.

   b. Replete with all the free samples you pick up from the cosmetics counter.

   c. Filled with coordinating items from your favorite makeup line.

   d. What makeup bag?

   e. Overflowing with all the different colored mascara, eye shadows, and eyeliners. You have a separate bag for lipsticks.

   f. Very small because you only wear lipstick, on special occasions.

5. Your hairstyle is …

    a. An easy-to-do version of the latest trend.

    b. A complicated version of the latest trend, with highlights.

    c. A shoulder-length bob.

    d. Very short or very long.

    e. Always changing; you like to try different colors and styles.

    f. A little scruffy; you never have time to get it cut.

6. Your choice of purses is …

    a. Just a wallet—who wants to lug all that stuff around?

    b. A large tote bag; you never know when you'll need an extra pair of pantyhose or a 12-ounce Diet Coke.

    c. A cute medium-size zippered purse.

    d. A backpack because you need to have your hands free.

    e. A brightly colored leather handbag with an overflowing wallet.

    f. A dog-eared planner with extra pens.

Now tally up how many *A* answers you gave, how many *B* answers, and so on. Whichever letter you choose most often defines your style:

    A—Classic and Simple

    B—Elaborate

    C—Down Home

    D—Earthy

    E—Wild Child

    F—Documenter

Keep reading to find a description of your style and a sample layout. This is your starting point. Let's take a look into each scrapbooker's likes and dislikes.

Classic and Simple

The simple scrapbooker likes clean, straight edges, owns few, if any, decorative scissors, and relies on a paper cutter and wide variety of colored cardstock to enhance her photos. She also uses stickers, die cuts, and page toppers, but only sparingly. "Less is more" is her motto.

Elaborate

The elaborate scrapbooker carries a cropper hopper full of her latest purchases so she can set up in an instant. She likes action on a page; plenty of stickers and fancy lettering. Eyelets and punches are favorites. Even if you aren't an elaborate scrapbooker, try to befriend one; she always has the latest clip art, computer programs, the newest pen styles, and up-to-the-minute magazines.

Down Home

The down-home person loves cute clip art, paper piecing, and Provo Craft stickers. Things with a homespun touch fill her scrapbook. She loves coordinating stickers and paper and enjoys stamping. Her scrapbook is consistent and relaxing, like reading a bedtime story.

Earthy

The earthy scrapbooker carries her supplies in a well-worn duffel bag and stays away from computer-generated scrapbooking, preferring to use more natural products. She likes muted colors and torn paper edges. She even goes so far as to make her own paper with interesting flowers and foliage garnered from her various outings. The earthy scrapper uses raffia to adorn her pages and uses her own handwriting to document the photos. This scrapbooker is creating an heirloom.

The Wild Child

The wild scrapbooker is flashy and hates rules. She doesn't need anyone to tell her what her style is! She likes bold colors and stickers and chooses patterns that are brash and bright. Her personality is evident on every page.

The Documenter

The documenter's goal is to get as many pictures as possible on a page, so she favors the 12 × 12 album that leaves plenty of room to journal on the layouts. Borders are popular, as are stickers. She is as concerned about preserving her family history as she is about creating artwork.

Once you've determined your primary style, you'll be able to streamline your shopping by focusing on the products you like. Of course you don't ever have to stick to one specific style. As a matter of fact, most people overlap into at least two categories, but by selecting what you generally like, you'll make your shopping expeditions easier and more purposeful. Why waste time looking at the newest stickers if you don't like them? You can head straight for the latest pen set if that's what you prefer.

Sticky Points

If your handwriting is illegible, you might want to use a computer to type up some of your stories. But be careful because most inkjet printers don't use archival or permanent ink. Your best bet is to use a laser printer, but if you don't own one, you can save the material to a disk and take it to your local copy center to print on a laser copier on acid-free paper. Whenever you make copies, ask that carbon-based ink or toner be used.

So Whaddya Need?

After you've decided which type best describes your individual style, it's time to determine what kind of scrapbooker you are. Do you have lots of time and few photos? Do you have mounds of photos and little time? Is money a factor? Keep reading to find a profile that suits you.

- ◆ **Hobbyist.** The hobbyist is someone who dabbles in many crafts and enjoys using her talents to decorate her living space. She is a social scrapbooker and shares her enthusiasm by starting scrapbooking groups. Don't miss a chance to go to one of her scrapbooking parties because she will be able to help you learn the latest techniques because she loves to share her craft!

- ◆ **World Wide Traveler.** This scrapbooker has been there, done that, and now wants to show it off! She needs methods to showcase her travel photos and brochures, as well as treasures she has gathered on her journeys. This scrapbooker's goal is to get the book done, as she enjoys the end product more than the process.

- ◆ **Empty Nester.** An empty nester has a house full of memories and a closet full of photos and partially completed albums. Overwhelmed by the huge task in front of her, she needs ideas for quick-and-easy pages and tips on preserving memorabilia, such as certificates and newspaper articles. This scrapbooker wants to finish her project so she can sit back and enjoy her efforts.

Sticky Points

If you're a scrapbooker with a lot of other projects going on, you'll need to be extra careful to keep your scrapbook supplies separate from your other projects. For example, don't confuse your regular stamp pad with your archival stamp pad or your stationery stickers for scrapbooking stickers; these products are not interchangeable.

◆ **Isn't He Adorable?** The proud parent. This mom or dad's kids are so cute that they take lots of photos to highlight all their kid's accomplishments. This parent enjoys scrapbooking as a way to relax with friends, and you'll often find her in an all-day workshop or even a 12-hour overnighter at her scrapbook store. Her scrapbooks are a work in progress.

◆ **Me and My World.** This teenager or child loves to record the fun events in his or her life: dances, birthday parties, field trips, school accomplishments, and best friends. With big dreams and a small budget, these scrapbooks have lots of personality.

Shortcuts

Don't know how to preserve all those certificates and newspaper clippings? If they're not acid-free, take them to your local copy store and copy them onto acid-free paper with a laser copier.

◆ **Career Track.** This person is so successful in the workplace that she has little time for scrapbooking. For her, scrapbooking is a way to relax and get away from it all. Her albums document her accomplishments, friends, and pets. Seeing a new product in the store spurs her on.

Now you're ready to go! You know what you like and how you like to do it. Keep this in mind the next time you go shopping.

But I'm Too Busy!

The key to having the time to scrapbook is knowing what you like and dislike, just as you have discovered in this chapter. Just imagine if there were only one clothing store that carried everything you ever needed—you wouldn't waste time shopping around in the mall because you'd go directly to that store, make your purchases, and be on your way. When you know your scrapbooking style, you can spend the time scrapbooking that you used to spend shopping. Try to set aside a chunk of time once a month or once a week for scrapbooking. Join a scrapbooking group, invite friends over, or go to a class. You will be surprised how much you can accomplish in this short amount of time.

The Least You Need to Know

◆ Are you a Wild Child, a Documenter, or an Earthy scrapbooker? Everyone has a different style and different needs.

◆ Once your style and needs are determined, you can save time and money.

◆ Make a favorites file to store interesting layouts and page ideas.

In This Chapter

◆ Discovering basic layout guidelines to help you create great pages

◆ Where to place accents to get the most for your money

◆ Does cutting your pictures sound like a nightmare to you? Ideas on using shapes in your scrapbooks

Chapter 16

Dress It Up! Layout Guidelines for Great Pages

I like to start my design techniques class by asking the participants why they chose to take the class and what it is that they are struggling with. The answers I hear are that people know how to use all the scrapbooking tools, but have a hard time putting everything together. They have difficulty actually laying out a page, so they ask for ideas and guidelines to keep page after page interesting. Many people complain that their pages are beginning to look the same—"Boring."

Scrapbooking is a kind of at-home crash course in graphic design. Once you know which products are available, and which are your style, you want to know the most interesting ways to lay out your pages.

Some people have a natural eye for decorating and graphic design—they put pictures and accents on a page and voilà—it looks terrific! Some of us don't have this intuition, but everyone will find that the design rules in this chapter will make a world of difference in your books. This chapter contains advice for creating a focal point, choosing shapes for your pages, placing accents, and adding your own signature touches. Remember, don't be too critical of yourself—enjoy this process!

From the Archives

The pioneer in page design is Stacy Julian, the author of *Core Composition,* published by Apple of My Eye. She has "the eye," and took it one step further to explain to others what works and why. You can see her work regularly in *Creating Keepsakes* magazine as she continues to teach us how to lay out our pages. She has personally taught me her techniques, and it has made a big difference in my pages. For more details on this topic, look for her informative book at your favorite scrapbook store or online site.

Keep It Simple—Basic Layout Guidelines

Start simple and then go from there.

Dive into the Pool

The first step in creating your layout should be selecting the photos to use. How many you have to select from depends on your *photo pool*. If you are a photo fanatic like me, you take as many pictures as possible. I have a father-in-law who prides himself on his picture-taking ability, and he always has great photos for me to add to my collection. I usually end up with a huge selection of photos, which gives me many scrapbooking options. If you aren't as lucky, you'll have to make do with the pictures you have.

Words for Posterity

A **photo pool** is the selection of pictures you have available to choose from.

People ask me how many pictures of any one event they should use. Guess what I say? That's right, there is no rule. If you want to use all ten rolls of Christmas photos, go ahead! When my sister and I went to Disneyland with my two older sons, we took four rolls of film, and the pictures turned out so great that I created an entire album of our Disneyland trip. You can choose what works best for you, but don't get stuck thinking that you must use every single photo from a given event. Remember, this is your family story, so use the pictures that best tell the story.

Shortcuts

For birthdays, try doing three or four double-page layouts showing the day's events, such as breakfast in bed, opening presents, and the kid's party.

From the Archives

Many families go a little crazy snapping shots of their firstborn and get a bit more lax when they have their second. To compensate, take some photos you have of your second (or third or fourth) child and add to them extra accents to create pages with different themes (even if the photos are from the same day). I took a roll of film of my second son swinging and playing in the backyard, and I used those pictures to fill in four or five pages with different themes. It's sneaky, but it works!

Choose a Theme

The next step is choosing a theme for your pictures. That way, you can select the accents and accessories that work best with the photos. If you end up with numerous photos within the theme, you can break the photos down into smaller categories. For instance, if you have a lot of pictures from Christmas 1995, you could divide them into categories such as hanging the stockings, decorating the tree Christmas morning, Christmas dinner, and so on.

This page tells you it was
a great day at the pool!

Focus on the Story

Now choose the focus of the story. Lay out your pictures and decide how you want to tell the story. When I am helping people in a class work on layouts, I ask them to get 6 to 10 pictures of an event and tell me about them. I like to talk with them about what is going on in the pictures, asking questions such as "What are you trying to show on these pages?" "What is your favorite picture?" and "Which picture best tells the story?" You can ask yourself these questions at home to help you decide how to present the story.

In this layout the focus is on the pictures,
what the child is doing—playing in the water.

Sticky Points

If you find a layout you like in a book, magazine, or other source, go ahead and copy it if you want, but be sure to personalize it by changing the colors and accents to match your photos.

Pick Colors and Accents

When you are sure of your storytelling direction, go to the next step—choosing colors. Colors affect not only the look of your layouts, but the mood. Select colors that reflect the mood of the events you are portraying by experimenting with different colors to get the feeling you want.

Selecting accents is my favorite part of scrapbooking. I suggest you choose embellishments that enhance your layout, not distract from it. To do this, keep in mind the story you are telling and the mood you have chosen. Pick accents that match your color scheme.

Sticky Points

The accent stage is where pictures can tend to get misplaced; for example, if you have the pictures out and can't find any accents to use with the photos. If you don't immediately find any accents to go with them, be careful that you don't put them away somewhere where you'll never see them again. Put your pictures in the proper place, even if you can't find something to match them right away.

Double the Pages, Double the Fun

When I refer to a spread or a double-page layout, I mean two pages, side by side that go together. Double-page layouts are pleasing to the eye because when a scrapbook is open you see both pages at the same time. Two cohesive pages display your pictures in the best possible way.

The double-page layout sends a message across with bright colors and bold lines.

If you don't have enough pictures to create a double-page layout but don't want to leave the other side blank, try using the same color scheme to give a look of consistency to the pages, even if the photos on the facing page are of a different event or theme. Another option is to use the additional page for journaling—we can always say something more about our photos (each is worth a thousand words, right?).

What's Your (Focal) Point?

The *focal point* is the most important composition tool for the scrapbooker. Every design has a focal point, whether it is the fireplace mantle in your living room or the island in a seascape painting. A focal point is something your eye is naturally drawn to, and you can manipulate the elements on your pages to highlight the focal point of your choice just as you would when decorating your living room. How do you do this? It's very simple, really! Emphasize the picture you chose as your favorite by treating it a little different than the rest.

Words for Posterity

A **focal point** is that element (usually a photo) where your eye goes first. Every layout has a focal point—be sure you decide what that focal point should be!

Following are some ways to make your focal point picture stand out:

◆ Place it at a different angle on the page—If all of the photos in the layout are tilted, place the focal point picture straight and parallel. Try the reverse, too.

◆ Double-mount the focal photo on an extra color of cardstock while leaving the other pictures single mounted.

◆ Use decorative scissors to trim around the cardstock the focal photo is mounted on and leave the other photos with straight edges.

◆ Try cutting the focal photo into a different shape than the others or placing your main accent near it.

◆ Journal around the focal photo or place the journaling under it to draw the viewer's attention there first.

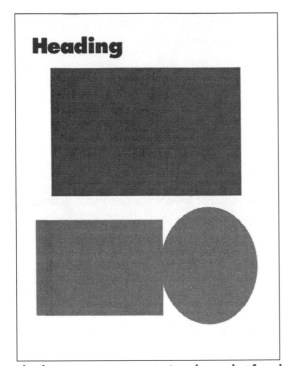

The large image on top is where the focal point picture is placed—it tells the story.

Create an eye-catching focal point by selecting two colors to double-mount your photo on.

The slight tilt of the photo draws you in.

The different edge on the focal point picture gets your attention.

Look at what using a different shape does to the focal point picture.

Everyone wants to read the story around this focal point picture to figure out what is going on.

By placing your main accent near your focal point photo, you create a winning page.

Shape Up!

Shapes are fun to use in your scrapbook. Using shapes in your books adds variety and interest to your pages. Look around your home and out in nature and see all of the shape variations that surround us. We need the variation in our scrapbooks, as well.

Not only is it great to cut photos into different shapes, you can also add shapes by using accents. For example, maybe you have rectangular pictures of you and your friends playing in the snow on a blue-and-white striped paper; to add shape, use accents that will contrast with the straight lines, such as snowflakes or a snowman.

If you do cut your photos into shapes, try not to cut too much out of pictures—sometimes the background of a photo has interesting or historical detail. For example, if you have an old picture of your grandparents standing by their car, leave the car in—it's not only interesting to see what they drove, it may help you date what year the photo was taken.

Although you want variety in your pages, you don't want to get too carried away. Try to achieve a balanced look by using equal amounts of shapes on each page, placing the shapes opposite each other on the pages, or placing similar-shaped photos at the points of a triangle across the layout.

Instead of cutting my photos into shapes I used a standard shape (circles) as an accent.

Shortcuts

You are the storyteller, so use the focal point photo to full advantage and make sure it is the one you want. When doing a Marine World layout, I chose to use a picture of my son with a huge grin on his face instead of the posed one of everyone in our group at the fountain. I did this because it best captured the events of the day.

Sticky Points

If you like trimming photos, make sure you cut only photos for which you have a negative or a duplicate.

Tips for Placing Accents

When working with accents, you want to add a certain type of feeling to your pages. Whether it is the close feeling of a family gathering or the elegance of a wedding, accents go a long way toward creating a mood.

A few tips for accent placement:

◆ Place the accent in a triangle shape on your page or pages.

◆ Group your stickers or punches with a purpose instead of randomly filling up space.

◆ Place the main accent near the focal point picture to draw attention to it.

◆ Try out the look before gluing on the page (if you are using stickers, experiment with placement positions before peeling them off their backing).

As in landscaping, interior design elements look good in odd numbers—especially in threes, as illustrated in this layout.

Look at the way these stickers are placed on the page. They reinforce the actions of the photo but don't overwhelm it. Notice the stickers are not covering every empty space on the page. Make good use of your negative space.

Sticky Points

Don't feel as if you have to use every sticker on the sheet that you purchased. Use the ones that complement your layout.

◆ Use realistically sized accents when possible—a little tiny strip of sticker grass under the photo of your niece standing in a meadow with grass up to her knees would seem out of proportion.

Negative Space

Another important layout principle is the wise use of negative space—that is, space on your pages that is free of pictures, captions, journaling, accents, borders, or any kind of decoration. The eye needs to have time to take everything in, and leaving portions of a layout empty prevents it from being too busy and frenetic. Negative space should be thought of as an accent in itself—study layouts that you like and note the use of empty space on the page.

This layout uses negative space well.

Shortcuts

Empty, or negative, space can serve effectively to highlight an item or allow the eye to absorb all the page elements.

The Least You Need to Know

◆ The look of your pages improves drastically when you create a focal point.

◆ By using a variety of shapes on your page you can create visual interest. Be careful not to shape or cut a photo with historical interest—never cut a one-of-a-kind photo.

◆ Place accents that will complement your layout and help tell your story.

◆ Negative space is a positive thing. An overabundance of design elements overwhelms the eye. Negative space encourages the eyes to wander and enjoy the images instead of darting all around, trying to take everything in.

In This Chapter

◆ Learn about the color wheel and how to use it

◆ How color affects the look and mood of your scrapbooks

◆ Tints, shades, value, and intensity—why these matter

◆ Choosing colors that work with your photos and please the eye

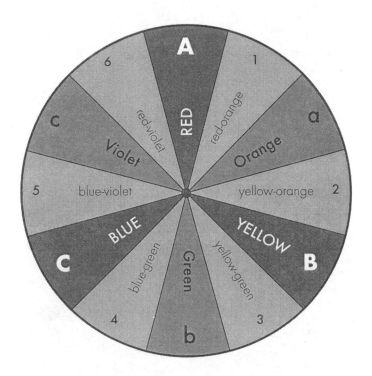

Chapter 17

Color It Yours

Color is a large factor in our scrapbooks. Color creates the mood for a page, highlights or distracts from photos, and portrays who we are. Often, the difference between a great page and a mediocre page is color. Most people who work on scrapbooks don't refer to the color wheel; they choose by instinct. If that works for you, great. But some people (like my sister) don't have an eye for color. She gets frustrated shopping for her layouts because she has such a hard time choosing colors. And some of her color combinations are awful—even she admits it! So I taught her how to use a color wheel, and it has helped her create better pages.

Because you want to keep the focus on your pictures, it's great to learn how to manipulate color. Don't be afraid to look to the experts for examples and inspiration. My favorite color combination comes from my favorite part of nature—the skies and trees. I use blue and green over and over again in my albums because it portrays the feeling that I want portrayed, and I find it very pleasing. Look at the art around you in paintings, architecture, and, of course, nature to give you color clues.

The ABCs of Color

Color is very important in setting a mood, both in the photographs you take and in the decorative elements of your scrapbook. Choices of color are everywhere, from the background paper you pick to the color of your embellishments. But what is color, exactly? If the last time you thought about this was in a physics class long ago, let's take a moment to go over a few color concepts.

ROY G. BIV

Light is the source of color. Pure white light is composed of all the colors the eye can see. You have probably seen this demonstrated with a prism—if you pass white light through a prism, the light refracts, or breaks apart, to show the rainbow spectrum, or ROY G. BIV. You remember him, right? The letters stand for the major colors, each with a different wavelength, that can be seen when white light is sent through the prism: red, orange, yellow, green, blue, indigo, and violet. The same thing happens when light passes through a drop of water—the water acts like a prism, and we see a beautiful rainbow.

Refraction

When light hits any surface, some colors are absorbed, while others are reflected. The colors that we can see (and that the lens of a camera sees) are the colors that are reflected. Imagine a big bouquet of sunflowers. The bright yellow petals of the flowers reflect only yellow wavelengths and absorb all the other colors, while the green leaves and stem reflect only green wavelengths. The reflections of the yellow and green wavelengths hit our eyes, and we see the glorious colors. An object looks black to our eyes when its surface absorbs all color wavelengths and white when the surface reflects all colors.

From the Archives

Even though colors can change depending on the kind of light we see them in, your brain automatically makes adjustments so that we see the colors as they are in bright light. For example, if you know that a shirt you are wearing is red and your jeans are blue, even if you are in a dim movie theater where your clothes look like almost the same color of brown, your eye will tend to "see" the pants and shirt as blue and red.

Colors in Nature

How can mood be affected by color? Researchers have shown that people react excitedly to "hot" colors, like red, orange, and bright yellow, and are soothed and calmed by what we think of as "cool" colors, like shades of blue and green.

Ever wonder why you are drawn to a certain item in your favorite department store? Wondering why you like to buy the expensive packaged food items instead of store brand? Color plays a role in everything we do, and those who are trying to sell us something have studied color and have it down to a science. They use color to get certain markets to purchase certain goods. You can find hundreds of books, online sites, and articles related just to the purchasing power of color. We can take their expertise and put it to work for us. Let's look at the basic colors in nature to see what mood they generate.

- **Blue.** When I was having my wisdom teeth out as a young adult, the oral surgeon's office was a blend of blues, from the furniture down to the fabric. He told me that blue is the most soothing and comforting color to humans—good to calm his anxious patients! Blues blend well with other colors, especially the bolder colors.

- **Green.** Green sends across feelings of growth. Everything around us in nature that is green is growing, and if it isn't growing, it changes color. The different hues of green work different ways. The softer colors are more mellow, and the darker colors are classic and go well with other classic colors.

- **Yellow.** Bright and sunny. Yellow, of course, generates energy and excitement, but use it in small doses because it can overwhelm and almost blind the eye.

I love to use yellow when I am doing summer pages with my kids running around and playing—it captures the energy of their childhood.

◆ **Red.** Red in nature screams bold and brave. This is a color that dominates everything it is in. Many fruits and vegetables are this color, and they look great growing on the green trees or plants. Green and red is often a natural combination in nature. Use these colors to show power and control.

Sticky Points _____

Don't get stuck using seasonal colors. If your Halloween photos are pink and purple, use those colors in your layouts—not orange and black.

Moods and Matching

People tend to associate certain colors with certain events and moods. For example, because people associate soft, calm, gentle colors with babies, baby clothes and other items are often made in pastels. By the same token, when people are making signs that they want others to see, they often choose bright, even electric colors, to get attention. People often match clothing to nature's seasonal colors—wearing fresh, light colors in the spring and summer, and richer, darker colors in fall and winter.

Unfortunately, though people often try to match with the seasons, they don't always match their socks to their pants. Certain colors don't seem to go together, but why don't those green, striped pants match those hot pink polka-dot socks? It's a matter of color and pattern. If you know anyone over five years old who leaves the house sporting an outfit like that, you may want to make them a copy of the next section!

From the Archives _____

Colors have tremendous cultural significance as well. In most Western cultures, black is the traditional color of mourning. In Eastern cultures, such as China, Japan, and Korea, however, it is white that is worn at funerals and times of mourning.

No Need to Reinvent the (Color) Wheel

If you have ever taken a basic art class, chances are that you have heard the term *color wheel* and have even seen one. I first learned about the color wheel in a high school interior design class, and I thought the concept was boring. I rebelled against the idea of obeying all these "rules" about picking colors. Now that I understand the ideas of color better, I find the color wheel useful, although the concepts can be a little confusing at first. Here I've adapted the basic rules of picking colors to apply to scrapbooking.

Words for Posterity _____

The **color wheel** has the main colors laid out to show their relationship and placement to one another. You can use the color wheel to create successful color combinations.

Decoding the Color Wheel

There are three basic color classes on the color wheel, which are referred to as follows:

◆ *Primary colors.* Names given in CAPITAL LETTERS.

◆ *Secondary colors.* Names given in lower-case letters.

◆ *Intermediate* or *tertiary colors.* These colors are numbered.

Words for Posterity

Red, yellow, and blue are called **primary colors**—they cannot be created; they just exist, which means that they are the base from which all other colors are created. **Secondary colors** are created by blending primary colors. Orange, green, and violet are the secondary colors created by mixing combinations of red, yellow, and blue. **Tertiary** (pronounced *TER-she-ary*), or **intermediate,** colors are blends of primary and secondary colors. Colors like red-orange and blue-green are tertiary colors.

Primary colors are the three colors from which all other colors can be made:

A = red

B = yellow

C = blue

These colors are of vital importance to artists. With paint in the three primary colors, plus white and black, an artist can create virtually any hue.

Secondary colors are made up of blends of the primary colors. They are

Orange (a) = Red (A) + Yellow (B)

Green (b) = Yellow (B) + Blue (C)

Violet (c) = Blue (C) + Red (A)

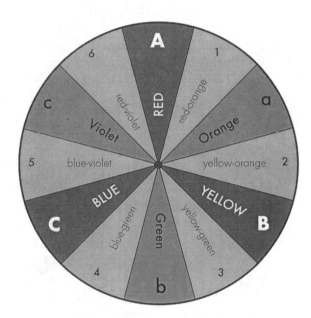

Tertiary, or intermediate, colors are made by mixing primary colors with secondary colors. Tertiary colors are indicated by numbers on the color wheel.

Red/Orange (1) = Red (A) + Orange (a)

Yellow/Orange (2) = Yellow (B) + Orange (a)

Yellow/Green (3) = Yellow (B) + Green (b)

Blue/Green (4) = Blue (C) + Green (b)

Blue/Violet (5) = Blue (C) + Violet (c)

Red/Violet (6) = Red (A) + Violet (c)

Tints and Shades

The next important thing to understand about color is how colors are affected by adding white and black. The basics are this: If you add white to a color, you are tinting it. A tint looks like a lighter version of a color. If you add black to a color, you are shading it. A shade looks like a darker version of a color.

> Color + black = shade
>
> Color + white = tint

Pastel (or "pale") colors are color tints. Pastel yellow is yellow that has white added to it; pastel blue is blue with white added. Pink is the name for the tint of red—that is, red mixed with white.

Color Intensity

Here are a few other terms related to color. You will sometimes hear the words *value* and *intensity* when people describe a color. These terms are somewhat related. The value of a color is determined by the amount of light or dark in it. Intensity is how true the color is to the primary colors. So the color red has more intensity than the color pink. Value is the component of color that describes its lightness or darkness.

Artists use intensity to evaluate the color of their paintings. Look at the works of two well-known artists, Picasso and Monet. Picasso used intense colors to create his bold paintings. Monet used a majority of less intense colors to create his soothing paintings. Picasso even had what is called his "Blue Period," where he almost exclusively used that color in every shade, tint, and variation possible.

Color Categories

The intensity of colors can be described either as bold or *muted*.

> ### Words for Posterity
>
> **Muted colors** are subdued tints or shades of colors and tend to be more suitable for backgrounds.

Bold colors are bright, high-intensity colors that demand attention. They reach out from the page and make you look at them. It is good to use these colors sparingly—when used as a background, they can dwarf your pictures.

On the other hand, muted colors are shades and tints of colors and are low-intensity, soothing colors. These colors are great as background colors, and using a lot of them is fine. The pictures will be emphasized when you use these colors.

> ### Shortcuts
>
> A painter might vary tints, shades, values, and intensities just by varying the amounts of colors that are blended together. Blending equal amounts of blue and yellow gives a true green color, which you can then shade or tint to your liking. Variations in amounts of color blended create variations in intensity.

You'll want to use combinations of bold and muted colors on your pages to create great effects.

Color for Success

If you don't read any other part of this chapter, make sure to look this one over. Following are color combinations based on the color wheel that are balanced and pleasing to the eye. Hewing too strictly to certain traditional combinations (like using all primary colors) can make your layouts a little predictable, so try being experimental with the complementary, analogous, and triadic combinations described in the following sections.

Colors that are called "complementary" combinations are opposite each other on the wheel:

- ◆ Red (A) and Green (b)
- ◆ Yellow (B) and Violet (c)
- ◆ Blue (C) and Orange (a)
- ◆ Red/Orange (1) and Blue/Green (4)
- ◆ Yellow/Orange (2) and Blue/Violet (5)
- ◆ Yellow/Green (3) and Red/Violet (6)

Analogous combinations are those that are next to each other on the color wheel. I'm using just the six basic colors to illustrate, but there are other combinations.

- ◆ Red (A) and Orange (a)
- ◆ Yellow (B) and Orange (a)
- ◆ Yellow (B) and Green (b)
- ◆ Blue (C) and Green (b)
- ◆ Blue (C) and Violet (c)
- ◆ Red (A) and Violet (c)

Triadic color combinations form a triangle on the wheel. This combination of colors can lend a sense of balance to your pages, though it can be quite stark in the primary or secondary forms. I prefer using them as tints of shades; for example, the pastel versions of green, orange, and violet are mint, peach, and lavender, respectively.

Following are all the triadic color combinations:

- ◆ Red (A), Yellow (B), and Blue (C)
- ◆ Orange (a), Green (b), and Violet (c)
- ◆ Red/Orange (1), Yellow/Green (3), and Blue/Violet (5)
- ◆ Yellow/Orange (2), Blue/Green (4), and Red/Violet (6)

Different values of the same color are referred to as monochromatic. An example of this is blue, navy, and pale blue. Blue is the primary color, navy is a shade of blue (remember, blue with black added), and pale blue is a tint (blue with white added). Monochromes can be quite impressive when used together.

Pleasing the Eye—Color Guidelines for Scrapbooking

Approaching color in your layouts will be most successful if you follow some basic color guidelines:

- ◆ You don't need to limit your colors to traditional choices. One Easter, for example, I dressed my four sons in navy blue outfits. When I went to make a page for these photos, the typical Easter pastel colors just didn't work.

◆ When choosing background paper, experiment with lots of the different colors available by holding your pictures against the choices to see what looks best.

◆ Use color to manipulate the story you are telling. Bold colors work well for a wild birthday party, while subdued colors might be better for an elegant anniversary party.

Look around you when considering color combinations. Check out the packaging at the grocery store or department store. Look through retail catalogs to see what colors go together in those. Every season, I look to the Gap to see what colors they are putting together this time. Sometimes, I would never have put together the combinations they try, but I am always impressed with how they put combinations together successfully. Use the experience of the professionals to get good color combinations.

Shortcuts

Match colors to the mood of your pictures. While pale blue is soothing and relaxing for a beach layout, yellow is energetic and spunky for fun at the circus.

Obviously, most of these "rules" are flexible—sometimes unexpected, unusual, or even outrageous combinations look great; sometimes, they are clashing disasters. And if children are working on scrapbooks, it's folly to expect them to pick colors that match—they won't, so let them color the way they want to. The great thing about scrapbooking is that you don't have to glue anything down in a hurry. Play around with layouts and color combinations until you are satisfied.

The Least You Need to Know

◆ If you don't have an "eye for color," a color wheel can be your Seeing Eye dog.

◆ Understanding a few properties of color can help you have the confidence to create very pleasing layouts.

◆ Shop with your photos to match paper and embellishments.

In This Part

Part 5

Great Pages for All Ages

An old Chinese proverb states, "The journey of a thousand miles begins with a single step." If completing your scrapbooks feels like a thousand-mile journey to you, you have plenty of company. You may have stacks of photos and don't know where to start. My suggestion to you? Theme pages that can be turned into an entire theme book. You will also want to investigate nonevent scrapbooking, the latest method of preserving your past. Follow the easy formula and you will experience success. Want to get the kids involved in this favorite pastime? Get some great suggestions for getting them started!

In This Chapter

- ◆ Theme books for big events
- ◆ Picture ideas you can't miss
- ◆ Don't forget to include the souvenirs in your travel album

Chapter **18**

Theme Albums

An old Chinese proverb states that "The journey of a thousand miles begins with a single step." If completing your scrapbooks feels like a thousand-mile journey to you, you have plenty of company. You may have stacks of photos and don't know where to start. My suggestion to you? Theme pages that can be turned into an entire *theme book*.

Theme books are scrapbooks that focus on one specific event or subject, such as weddings or holidays. Theme books are great projects for beginners, because you don't have to buy a lot of different paper and embellishments, and you get a great feeling of completion every time you finish one.

If you are ready to tackle some of your irreplaceable photos, I have a few suggestions for you. First, make color copies of one-of-a-kind photos, certificates, and documents and use the copies in your scrapbooks so that you've always got a back-up if you aren't satisfied with your work. Store the originals in acid-free envelopes in a safe place, maybe a safe deposit box. Next, if these are professionally made photos, you probably spent a lot of money on them, so you don't want to obscure them with stickers and embellishments. Last, keep it simple. These are photos that stand on their own, and too many embellishments diminish rather than enhance their impact.

Words for Posterity

Theme books are scrapbooks devoted to a specific theme such as family traditions, vacations, or holidays.

Around the World

It's human nature to want to get away and explore other places, and travel and vacations are a great escape. They are a naturally colorful topic for scrapbooks, providing exciting visuals, lots of new experiences and people to write about, and great souvenirs you'll certainly want to save.

When traveling around the world, one discovers cultures and landmarks that speak for themselves. Display these photos in scrapbooks to enjoy and treat them as artwork.

Shortcuts

Make sure to get some pictures of yourself when you travel. Too often, the photographer gets back from a trip to find that there is not a single photo of him or her in the bunch! To keep your pictures from being an impersonal travelogue, make sure you ask your travel companions or friendly people on the streets to snap pictures of you.

Here are some photos you must have:

◆ Trip preparations

◆ Arrival in different cities

◆ All of the places you visited

◆ Your transportation

◆ Exotic places where you dined

◆ People you met

◆ Landmarks

If you have traveled overseas, you'll most certainly bring back a load of pictures of beautiful and historical landmarks. Some, such as the Eiffel Tower or Buckingham Palace, are world famous and instantly identify the country you visited. Others, such as the tiny old covered market you happened on in Egypt, are places that are off the beaten path and that you don't ever want to forget. Make sure the embellishments don't detract from the scenery in your photos. Not many embellishments are available for travel, so be selective when choosing designs for your layouts.

Shortcuts

Create a title page for your travel scrapbook by marking your journey. Use your travel itinerary or highlight your route on a map. This is a great starting point.

This layout highlights one way to add memorabilia to your layout. Remember, memorabilia is a great way to accent those travel photos.

Cruisin' Around

Cruise vacations have their own charm—they can be super relaxing (sunning on the deck) and very exciting (dropping the passengers off in interesting and beautiful sites). If you love cruises, like my sister-in-law Linda, a cruise connoisseur, here are some ideas for making a special book about a cruise trip. Whether you've gone on one cruise or a dozen, or are thinking about taking one someday, try to get some photos of the following:

- Boarding the boat
- Sunning on deck
- New friends
- Eating at the buffet
- Loosening your belt after the buffet
- Exciting ports of call
- The crew
- Your tour of the ship
- Your cabin

Shortcuts

I have seen pages where the letters one has received on a journey were used to create interesting and personal background paper. Try this; you will be pleased with the results.

When I think of cruising, I think of the brilliant blues and greens of the ocean. Emphasize these with a selection of bright colors to use with your photos.

Shortcuts

Because cruises are famous for their endless cuisine, make sure you take pictures of the food and see if you can take home a copy of the menu to add to your book.

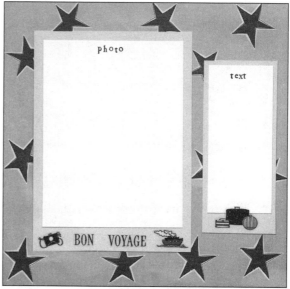

A fun template for a travel layout.

I Do—Wedding Albums

I spent more money on my wedding photographs than the rest of the wedding combined. I didn't mind skimping on the food or even the flowers, but the photographs had to be well done. I have never regretted that decision. After spending so much money, I wanted my scrapbook to look great.

While your photographer will take many posed and candid shots, be sure to assign some of your friends to take some photographs of the festivities. Some people even distribute disposable cameras among their guests for this purpose.

If you have yet to take photos of a wedding, here are some shots to be sure to get:

- Guests eating and enjoying themselves
- Children in the wedding party letting loose
- The spread of food and cake
- The decorations before the people come
- People's expressions during the ceremony
- Aunt Irene doing the "funky chicken" on the dance floor
- The stash of wedding gifts
- Bride and groom leaving for their honeymoon
- The cutting of the cake
- Musical performers

These pictures would be fun to have, too:

- The getaway car decorated with shaving cream and tin cans
- Parents of the couple dancing together
- Flower girl sleeping on her mom's lap
- The groom's happy face
- The bride sneaking away from the reception line to grab something to eat
- The girls fighting to catch the bridal bouquet
- The messy reception hall after the guests have left
- Father of the bride trying not to cry

The first step with this type of scrapbook is to decide on a theme. While your wedding is the main theme, the style and location of the wedding can determine the look of the scrapbook. If you got married in a garden, for example, floral paper is a natural choice. If your wedding was a black-tie affair complete with a sit-down dinner, you'll probably want to use a more elegant paper, such as embossed, vellum, or handmade. By the same token, make sure the embellishments you use are in keeping with the style of the book.

The use of elegant paper, soft colors, and minimal accents create an ideal wedding page.

Sticky Points

A scrapbooking rule of thumb is never to cut pictures if you don't have the negatives. This is especially important when doing wedding pictures.

Baby Days

Does anyone know exactly when a baby stops being a baby? One mom I know refers to her 16-year-old daughter as her baby. But babies grow up, and for the sake of this chapter, I will refer to babies as children up to one year old.

My top advice for you is to take tons of pictures during that first year. Babies change so fast that you need a lot of film to document all of it. When my twins were born three years ago, I was in such a daze that I didn't have film in the camera the day they were born! I am lucky enough to have a father-in-law who takes pictures all the time, so he gave some to us. But don't let that happen to you!

Must-have pictures to document baby's first year:

- Baby with Mom and Dad for the first time
- Coming home from the hospital
- First time in bassinet
- First bath
- First outing
- Baby meeting grandparents and extended family
- First solid food
- Baby smiling
- Baby sleeping
- Favorite toy
- Baby's special blanket

Pictures that are fun to have:

- Photo of Mom on the delivery day outside of the hospital (try to capture the weather) with the hospital's sign in the background.
- The doctor and nurse who delivered the baby
- Mom all worn out after the delivery
- The baby on the scale
- Baby meeting siblings
- Dad asleep in rocking chair with baby
- Big brother or sister giving baby a bottle

- All the gear you pack into your diaper bag for a one-hour outing
- The dishes piled up in the sink
- The baby shower

Shortcuts

Family historians recommend that you take at least one roll a year of black-and-white film. Black and white can pick up details that color can't capture, and you'll be thrilled to look back on these photos.

Of course, some embellishments just have to be included in your baby book, such as the bottle, carriage, baby feet and hands, and baby bibs, but don't stop with just these old favorites. Look for some medical embellishments to go along with baby's first trip to the doctor or use some dishes to accent baby's first meal.

The soft hues of colors combined with the focal point position of photos work well to create a sweet baby layout.

Man's and Woman's Best Friends

If you're an animal lover, you have at least one pet who is a member of your family. My sister has two cats who she takes everywhere with her. She buys them special food and collars and loves to photograph them in various poses. If you've got pictures of your pet piling up, why not put them in a scrapbook for everyone to enjoy? The kids will love to join in on a pet book, so get them involved.

If you've had your pet for a while, you probably have many snapshots to choose from, but just in case, here are some photo suggestions.

Here are some pictures you must have:

◆ The day you brought your pet home

◆ Your pet at the veterinarian's office

◆ The place your pet sleeps, whether it's in a basket, a box, or your bed

◆ Pet's favorite meal

◆ Pet playing with you and other family members

◆ Going on walks with your pet

◆ Pet riding in your car

◆ Outings with pet—camping, beach, or lake

◆ Pet-sitter

◆ Animal friends of your pet

◆ Pet romping in the yard

Don't forget these:

◆ Pet birthday parties

◆ Pet during holiday festivities

◆ Pet wearing those horrible collars after getting stitches

◆ Pet wearing brand new collar

◆ You and your pet sleeping

◆ Pet wearing sunglasses and hat

◆ Pet waiting for you to get home

◆ The kids dressing up your pet in doll clothes

You can find all sorts of animal accents, from dogs and cats to farm animals to zoo animals.

Capturing your furry friend's uniqueness is imperative—this example layout will give you some ideas!

Pass It on, Pass It Down

My mom has only about five photos of her childhood. One of them is missing a corner, and another has a crease down the middle. If you are luckier than me and have lots of old family photos to preserve, you'll want to read this section.

From the Archives

You might want to consider having damaged photos fixed at a photo lab in which the employees are proficient with Photoshop. This program can make a photo look like it was never damaged.

If you are making a book that uses mostly older photos, keep embellishments to the bare minimum because they often clash with the classic-looking photos. Instead, use muted borders and some journaling to tell the story behind the pictures.

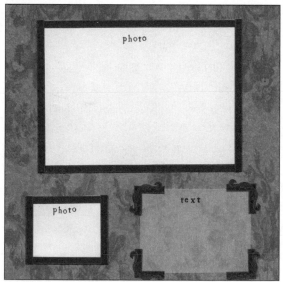

This layout illustrates how maintaining a minimalistic look enhances heritage photos.

A Few of Their Favorite Things

Kids have many favorites, whether it's a favorite color or a favorite food or a favorite toy—and it's fun to make a favorites book. A great way to start this project is to ask your child all sorts of questions.

Here are some questions to get you started. Encourage your child to think of more favorites. Remember, you want this to capture your child's unique personality and that may mean including your child's favorite potato chip flavor!

◆ What is your favorite food? Dessert?
◆ My favorite family activity is _____.
◆ My favorite room in the house is
   _____.
◆ What is your favorite memory?
◆ What is your favorite flower?
◆ My favorite movie is _____.
◆ My favorite vacation is _____.
◆ What is your favorite flavor of ice cream?

Must-have pictures for a favorites book:

◆ Child with best friends
◆ Wearing favorite outfit
◆ Eating favorite cereal
◆ Participating in favorite activity
◆ Playing outside during her favorite season
◆ Singing his favorite song
◆ Drawing with his favorite color crayon
◆ Playing a favorite game
◆ Reading a favorite book
◆ Cooking a favorite meal

To remind yourself to record your children's favorites each year, create a favorites list and have them fill it out on their birthday every year. It will be fun for you and them to look back and see what they used to like.

Easy as ABC (and 1, 2, 3)

Another fun project is an ABC book. You can make a theme ABC book, as in "ABC at the Circus," beginning with "A is for acrobat" and going on through to "Z is for zebra," for example.

Here is the list I used for my "ABCs in Action" book.

A: Aunts coming to visit

B: Bouncing on the trampoline

C: Crying over spilt milk

D: Daredevil stunts

E: Eating eggs for breakfast

F: Frosting a cake

G: Giggling

H: Hide and seek

I: Itchy chicken pox

J: Jumping on the bed

K: Kicking the soccer ball

L: Laughing at the movies

M: Making mud pies

N: Nestling under a blanket

O: Opening presents

P: Putting puzzle pieces together

Q: Quitting for the day

R: Running to first base

S: Sliding down the water slides

T: Taking the dog for a walk

U: Using the lawn mower

V: Vandalism cleanup

W: Waking Mom up early

X: X-raying a broken bone

Y: Yawning on the bus

Z: Zooming around the schoolyard

The fun thing about these books is you can focus on your children and highlight the items they enjoy. For a simpler task, try doing a number book. You could include pictures of their favorite things they can count (one jelly bean, two stuffed animals, three wooden blocks, and so on).

Birthdays!

I used to take so many birthday pictures that I didn't know what to do with them. I mean, who can resist taking at least three pictures of your child opening each present, five of him blowing out the candles on the cake, and a dozen of him playing with his new toys? If you are in the same predicament, here are my suggestions:

Let's say that your daughter Linda is turning four next week, and you are planning a party with some of her friends. Here is a list of must-have photos:

◆ Linda in her party dress

◆ Linda opening her gifts

◆ The birthday cake with the candles lit

◆ The birthday girl's cheeks filled with air as she gets ready to blow out the candles

◆ The extended family gathered to celebrate Linda's big day

◆ The friends at her party

◆ The stack of unopened presents

◆ Linda greeting her party guests (*that* will be cute!)

◆ The children playing musical chairs, pin the tail on the donkey, and blind man's bluff

- Linda unwrapping her gifts
- Linda holding up four fingers
- Linda spilling red punch on her birthday dress
- All the party guests gathered around Linda
- Linda fighting with her sister over her new toys
- Pictures of the apartment after all the kids have left and before you've cleaned up
- The birthday girl fidgeting while Mom tries to fix her hair for the party
- Mailing or delivering party invitations
- Linda having a breakdown from all the excitement
- Linda's sister poking her finger in the frosting
- Finally, after the party, Linda tucked in bed with her new doll in one hand, her crumpled party hat in the other

Although these photo ideas are based on a young child's birthday party, you can easily adapt them for teenagers and adults. Your husband will appreciate the picture of him blowing out fifty candles on his cake!

If you already have pictures but need some fresh ideas on how to display them, remember that many of the classic birthday embellishments span generations. Candles, party hats, presents, and confetti can be used on pages for people from 8 to 80.

A Scrapbook for All Seasons

Another great scrapbook theme is seasons. We measure the passing of life and milestones by noting the seasons, and as each season comes around again, we are reminded of years past and the traditions we participate in. It's important to record these times.

Spring Has Sprung

These are some must-have photos for spring:

- Dressed up in Easter finery
- Easter baskets
- Egg hunts
- Dyeing eggs (and hands and clothes!)
- Your child holding the Mother's Day gift he made for you
- You and your mom on Mother's Day
- Packing up sweaters and scarves until next winter
- A green St. Patrick's Day dinner
- Bouquet of Secretary's Day flowers
- Planting a vegetable garden
- Baby birds in their nests

Here are some other fun spring photos:

- Splashing in mud puddles
- Your dog shaking off the rain inside your living room
- The first tulip
- Kids holding handfuls of dandelions they brought you
- Pushing your kids on swings in the park
- Making mud pies
- Rainbows
- The kids tromping through your freshly planted flower bed
- Dad sliding down the slide

Hazy, Lazy, Crazy Days of Summer

Here are some ideas to get you started on that album capturing all the fun times of summer:

- Whether you've got a built-in pool or a teeny inflatable one, snap those swimming shots
- Watching the Fourth of July parade
- Water fights when the sun is sizzling
- Backyard camp outs
- Family picnics
- Wading at the beach
- Building sand castles
- Roasting marshmallows over a campfire
- Trips to the ice-cream shop
- Playing hopscotch in the backyard

Here are some unusual photos that will make your scrapbook more personal:

- Those adorable curb-side lemonade stands
- Kids with Popsicle-stained faces
- Fourth of July fireworks
- Sunburns (They'll remind you to wear sunscreen next year!)
- The towel rack crowded with dripping swimsuits
- The ice cream truck stopping by your house
- The lawn that got scorched during the heat wave
- Your bathtub full of sand after a day at the beach
- Another failed attempt at homemade ice cream

Here are some quick tips for photographing fireworks:

1. Have a tripod—this can't be stressed enough—if you don't have one, ignore the rest of this list.
2. Regardless of your film speed (but, yeah, should be at least 400), set your SLR for B (bulb), which will enable you to control how long the shutter stays open.
3. Have a hat or dark piece of paper (or anything wide and dark).
4. Decide how many fireworks you want on one frame.
5. Hit the release button while holding the hat over the lens.
6. Remove the hat when the fireworks are exploding, and leave the hat off for as long as you want the streaks to last on your frame.

Go Jump in the Leaves!

Here are some ideas for must-have fall pictures:

- Halloween costumes
- Playing in the fall leaves
- Thanksgiving feast
- Harvesting the vegetables
- Pumpkin patch
- Carving pumpkins
- Carving the Thanksgiving turkey
- Raking leaves
- Making caramel apples
- Going on hay rides

These autumn pictures are fun to have:

◆ School Halloween parade

◆ Putting on the clown makeup

◆ Candy sack filled with candy

◆ You and your friends going off to a costume party

◆ The kitchen before the Thanksgiving dishes are cleaned up

◆ Peeling mounds of apples for the apple pies

◆ Going to the Thanksgiving parade

Winter Wonderland

Here are some classic photo ideas for "the most wonderful time of the year":

◆ Family in front of the Christmas tree

◆ Lighting the Menorah

◆ Exchanging gifts

◆ Baking goodies

◆ Frolicking in the snow (no matter how old you are!)

◆ Frosting cookies

◆ Family decked out in holiday finery

◆ A visit to Santa Claus

◆ Holiday meals

◆ Ice skating or sledding

And how about these:

◆ Car covered in snow after the tenth snowstorm

◆ Your kids undecorating the tree

◆ Your two-year-old licking frosting off the cookies

◆ Kitty cat playing with the kitty toys in her stocking

◆ Kids coming in from the snow with red noses

◆ Drinking hot cocoa

◆ Pictures of your favorite gifts and the person who gave them to you

◆ Dad wearing that silly tie the kids gave him

◆ Wrapping paper mess

◆ Baby crying on Santa's lap

◆ Kids asleep with their new toys

Now that you've got the photos, let's dress them up. I love all the holiday accents, such as Christmas trees, stockings, menorah, carolers, ivy, and party hats.

The Least You Need to Know

◆ Children grow up, but you can keep them forever young by scrapbooking.

◆ Be sure to photograph the everyday events, as well as special occasions.

◆ There is no such thing as too many baby pictures!

◆ The theme of ABCs and 1, 2, 3s for children's books provides you with a structure, but gives you lots of room for creativity.

◆ Keep the colors of spring in your scrapbook and capture the dog days of summer by making a seasonal scrapbook.

◆ Use colors that bring out the colors of your travel photos.

◆ Take pictures of the people you visit, as well as the landmarks.

◆ Enjoy your wedding day over and over again through pictures—don't forget to scrapbook those anniversary shots.

In This Chapter

◆ Why a dedication page is crucial for your viewers' understanding of the scrapbook

◆ Keeping a scrapbook that goes beyond everyday events to your family values, photos you love, and life-changing experiences

◆ Follow the format for a quick and easy way to create a theme scrapbook

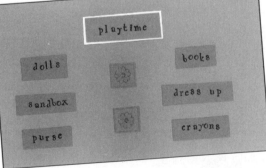

Chapter 19

Creating a Theme Album Step by Step

For those of you who don't want to tackle those years of photos stuffed in drawers and boxes throughout your home, there is another solution for you. Decide on a theme for your scrapbook and gather the appropriate materials and pictures. Flip through your photos, look at your journal, and jot down a few ideas for a theme album.

Step by Step to a Theme Album

There is a very easy-to-follow formula for this new scrapbooking concept—you can find the long version in the magazine that is devoted to this concept, *Simple Scrapbooks;* go to their website, www.simplescrapbooksmag.com, or pick up a magazine. I'm giving you the short version in this chapter.

As you can imagine, the ideas are endless and anyone can find a topic to create a theme scrapbook. To best illustrate this process, I have selected some theme scrapbooks I did, and as we go through each step, I'll illustrate with my theme scrapbooks. To see a more detailed format pick up the latest issue of *Simple Scrapbooks* magazine and see their pull-out card.

Focus

This is the most interesting part of the project. You decide what you want the message of your theme scrapbook to be. You might want to teach your kids your family values, or you might want to document the history of your garden. A few questions to ask as you define your focus could be:

◆ What emotion do I want the viewer to feel?

◆ What story am I trying to tell?

◆ What resources are available for me to compile this album?

Once you define your focus, you will be ready to proceed to the next step. In the theme scrapbook I show in this chapter, my focus was to capture my niece's, Emmie's, world. I wanted to present this album as a gift to Emmie's mother, my sister, as a simple way to remember her daughter's first year. When your focus is defined, you need only a few pictures that capture the important aspects—in this case, Emmie's personality. Following are some basic ideas for theme scrapbooks:

◆ Namesake album

◆ Accomplishments

◆ Career highlights

◆ Favorite family recipes

◆ Holiday traditions

◆ Halloween costumes

From the Archives

Photographers have been creating theme scrapbooks for years. They traditionally have placed their showcase photos in personalized books that display a grouping of their photographs. Oftentimes, they will create a hand-bound book that matches and coordinates with the photos.

Shortcuts

Imagine 50 years from now what you would want people to know about your family's life.

Framework

This unique aspect of a theme scrapbook is borrowed from the more traditional books. As the author, you can create any type of framework pages that you want. I am going to suggest three types:

◆ **Title page.** As the first page in the album, this sets the stage.

◆ **Dedication page.** Who this album is for, why it was created, and what you hope viewers will take from it.

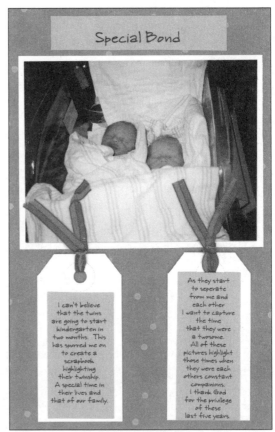

Dedication page.

◆ **Table of contents page.** This is where you break up your album into categories. You can use different accents or colors to differentiate between the sections.

Table of contents.

Shortcuts

Look in your favorite storybook for frame-work ideas.

Materials File

Ask yourself what available products will help you reinforce the photo story you're sharing. You want to be driven by the photos, not the products.

Words for Posterity

A **materials file** is a gathering of all items used in creating your theme album, excluding photographs. It should include all of your paper, accents, and sketches.

Some tips on choosing a color scheme:

◆ A good rule of thumb is to use three main colors with two neutrals.

◆ Use your color scheme to reinforce the mood of the album.

◆ Add two to three patterns that work with your colors.

Materials file excluding album.

Accent Selection

A couple tips on selecting accents:

◆ Use accents that reinforce the theme or focus of the album.

◆ What are your available resources, time- and money-wise? Do you want to use accents that are pre-illustrated or do you want to hand make your own?

Layout Design

Look through magazines and books to find some layouts that you like—use these as a guide to sketch out how you want your layout to look. Remember, you can vary the look of your layout if that suits you—it helps to have a few standard sketches to pull from and keep a consistent look throughout the album. Consider these points as you compile your layout sketches:

- What is your completed page size going to be?
- What shapes are you going to use?
- How will you add texture to your layouts—pattern paper, accents, etc.?

Shortcuts

You can purchase a book that is full of layout sketches, *My Creative Companion*, directly from www.creatingkeepsakes.com or in any scrapbook store.

Journaling

Journaling is oftentimes an intimidating part of scrapbooking. The secret is to find a way to use words to help tell the story in a manner that is doable for you. You can try the traditional journaling method that includes the who, what, why, when, and how questions, or try some other methods.

List journaling is a fun way to share words without worrying about grammar and sentence structure. List your feelings, favorites, events that occurred … anything that is applicable.

You can also try to document actual conversations. I enjoy writing down what my kids say, especially when they are toddlers.

Another method to try is the storybook method. You write down the entire story from beginning to end, then break it up so you have some of the story on each page. This works well to keep the reader reading the entire album. For some other methods try the www.gracefulbee.com link to journaling.

Shortcuts

Carry a journaling notebook with you to write down notes or ideas as they come to you.

Album Selection

The next step is to select your album size and style. You can find virtually any size or create your own. Here are some helpful questions to consider as you select your album:

- How am I going to display this album? Is it going to be available for reviewing at all times, or am I going to take it out for special occasions such as holidays?
- Do I want to be able to add more pages to the album?
- What size album is going to best suit my layout design?
- Do I need the pages to have sheet protectors on them?
- What is my budget for this album?

You can pick up the basic albums at your local scrapbook store or craft store. If you are interested in more specialty type of albums, check out these websites:

www.albumsource.com (very large selection and variety)

www.aspinaloflondon.com (beautiful handcrafted albums, English style)

www.centuryphoto.com (will imprint your album cover)

www.mollywest.com (inspiring collection of hand-bound albums)

www.handmadepapergifts.com (you can select the paper for the cover, ribbon for binding, and more)

www.gerryscrafts.com (handmade fabric albums, great selection)

www.timelesstapestry.com (assortment of tapestry albums in a variety of sizes)

www.creativememories.com (the original)

www.closetomyheart.com (postbound albums—the pages lay flush with each other)

Album for Emmie.

Finished Project

Now you are ready to cut and paste. Start with a blank work space with everything on hand. Turn on some music and put it all together. It is helpful to save the items from your materials file in a designated spot if you plan on adding more pages to the album. If you plan on storing, remember to store it where the temperature remains consistent and in a dust-free environment.

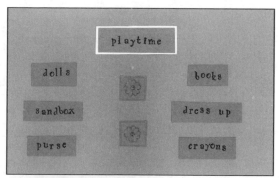

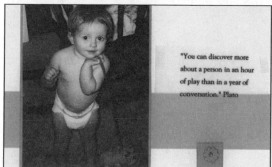

Some finished pages.

Sticky Points

It's helpful to note in your materials file the store where you purchased the items in case you run out.

The last page.

The Least You Need to Know

◆ Use your color scheme to reinforce the mood of your album.

◆ Look to nonevent scrapbooking to become the new trend.

◆ Try a variety of journaling methods to capitalize on your journaling.

In This Chapter

◆ Creative fun for kids using scrapbooking materials

◆ Projects that parents and kids can do together

◆ Tips for helping kids take great pictures

◆ Working safely with kids

Scrapbooking Isn't Just for Grown-Ups

Kids love to make scrapbooks. In fact, one of the greatest parts of my job is teaching kids' scrapbooking classes—partly because kids don't have the same inhibitions that adults do and get really creative with their books, and partly because I get to act silly, and the kids appreciate all the fun things we do in class. Kids like to scrapbook their vacation photos, photos of friends, and anything else they can think of.

Recently, we were doing baby pictures at a kids' class. I loved listening to the children describe what was going on in their baby pictures. I imagined their parents going through the pictures with them and telling their children what they remembered about them. One little girl described an incident where she got into her mother's lipstick and, even though her mother was frustrated, she took pictures of her. She did the cutest page with these pictures, and she thought it was great her mom captured her on film.

This chapter gives tips on scrapbooking with kids, as well as fun projects to do with them. If you are interested in teaching kids, there are some suggestions on how to make teaching scrapbooking fun with games and goodies.

Kids Are Scrappers, Too

Sometimes, children see the whole picture of a project better than we do because they don't feel the same pressure to "get it done" that many of us do. Kids truly enjoy the process of making a scrapbook as much as the product. All children need is some encouragement and the freedom to use their own style. It's great when adults and children can work on scrapbooks together—either on the same book or each on an individual book.

If you are setting up supplies for some kids you know (or if you are a kid and you want to get yourself set up), here are some things you'll want to get prepared from a teaching curriculum I created for a kids' basic scrapbooking class:

◆ **Be prepared.** Have supplies organized in some sort of container.

   1. To start with, you need scissors, paper, pens, accents, glue, and an album with sheet protectors.

   2. Have pictures sorted according to event, such as a birthday party, trip to the zoo, or best friends.

   3. Make sure you have a clean work space.

◆ **Get started.**

   1. Pick a theme for the pictures you are working on if possible (such as a camping trip, vacations, school, birthday, or friends).

   2. Help the child choose a color scheme, encouraging him or her to stick with three or four colors that match the photos.

◆ **Shop 'til you drop.**

   1. You need to have a plan when shopping with your child. Bring only a few photos to the store and don't stay too long; you want this to be fun, not stressful!

   2. Find embellishments that match the color scheme the child has picked.

Colors go great with the child's perception of the activity.

◆ **Cut and color.**

   1. If you want to trim your photos, encourage your child to match the pattern of the scissors to the theme of the page.

   2. Mount your photos on coordinating cardstock and trace and color borders.

   3. If desired, your child can draw some pictures to go along with the photos. This is especially good if the child is too young to write.

You can tell this child loves to cut.

◆ **Put it all together.** Teach the child a few designing guidelines to follow so they will be happy with their creative results and want to do more.

◆ **Write it down.** I think this can be the most important part of the scrapbooking process. It is amazing what your child remembers about different events.

1. Ask questions and encourage your child to write responses in his or her own words.

2. Some children are self-conscious about their penmanship and are reluctant to use their own writing. A good compromise is to have a title and date for the page, and you write in the text. That way, you still get their cute lettering, but your child is happy, too.

3. If your child is too little to write, make sure you write down the things they tell you. Put the writing into a protector and keep on going.

Sticky Points

Children don't have the same concept of time as we do, so give them plenty of time to shop and see what all of their options are. You will be surprised at what they can come up with.

This child shows and writes what some of his favorite activities are.

Shortcuts

Scrapbooking with kids is a two-step process: organizing and selecting items to use on a page and putting it all together. Depending on the age of the kids, it can be hard to do it all at once, so do it in parts. Place selected items with pictures in a protector, and you and the children will be ready to go.

From the Archives

Once, a mother of six attended one of my scrapbooking classes. At one point, she was so overwhelmed with compiling her family's pictures into a scrapbook that she taught her two oldest children how to do it. Now they do most of the scrapbooking, and even some of the younger kids are involved.

Color Control and Easy Extras—Kid's Guide to Layouts

I also teach a kids' design class. Here are some basic design rules for kids.

◆ **Eye catcher.** Every design needs a focal point and so do scrapbook pages. Carefully choose the picture that you want to be the focal point, usually the one that tells the story the best way possible.

◆ **Shapes.** Shapes are great for kids' pages, but encourage them to use shapes sparingly. Remember, if they don't want to cut their pictures into shapes, they can add interest to their pages with accents that are shapes.

◆ **Cool colors.** Kids are often attracted to bright, bold colors. Help the kids to make their pages look cool—not too many and not too few. I think three or four colors is plenty. Teach kids to use colors to match the pictures and the mood of the pictures.

◆ **Theme.** Remember to use the book's theme as the finishing design so that everything works well together and tells a unified story.

◆ **Extras.** Help kids remember that accents are extras. You don't have to use them on every page, and too many detract from your photos.

Kid focal point layout. The accents in this layout keep the focus on the photo, creating a focal point.

See how the use of shapes in this photo doesn't overdo the layout, but rather adds interest.

Sticky Points

When working with kids, give them the basic rules and let them go to work. They want to have fun, and if you are critical or push them too hard, they won't enjoy it. So if Susie wants to put a dozen Little Mermaid stickers on one page, let her!

You can tell that this little girl thinks she is a princess.

Picking Pineapples and Making Friends—Fun Projects

While it's good to give your kids some tools and set them loose, sometimes it's a good idea to provide them with a little structure and a theme. Here are some kid-friendly projects:

◆ **My Best Friends.** Kids can use all of the pictures they take of their friends and class pictures that they get every year. Let them make a page with these photos, listing what they like about their friends and the fun things they do together.

◆ **Family Tree.** You can purchase some of the preprinted family tree paper or you can make your own. Let the children use pictures if possible to show as many generations as you have. This is a great project for any child.

◆ **10 Things I Want to Do When I Grow Up.** Did you ever make one of those lists where you wrote down that when you grew up you'd like to go parachuting, pick pineapples, or be an astronaut? This is fun to put in a scrapbook. A variation of this is "10 Things I Want to Do Right Now." (Kids might include staying up all night, playing Nintendo all day, and eating candy for dinner! Whatever they choose, this is a fun project for them and fun for you—maybe you can even make some of those things come true for them.)

◆ **Make simple gifts.** Kids love to give homemade gifts to grandparents and others. Try giving them some of your leftover supplies and letting them create a gift that could be preserved forever. My kids have made bookmarks, cards, pictures of themselves with the loved one on a cute scrapbook page, a set of thank you cards, a recipe book, mini-scrapbooks, stories, gift bags, gift tags, and more.

◆ **Resource book.** Use this paper-crafting time to compile resource notebooks. Try making a kid-friendly recipe book with your child or make a baby-sitting book (see accompanying examples).

Make dividers for a baby-sitting book.

Kid's Project #1—Paper Dolls That Fish and Swim

You need the following supplies:

- Glue
- Straight-edge scissors
- Scraps of paper for clothes
- Paper dolls (if you don't want to create your own pattern, you can purchase these precut or die cut them yourself)

Paper dolls in a scrapbook can reinforce your photo story. If the pictures are of you at the beach, put your paper dolls in bathing suits and have them doing what you are doing. It's fun to duplicate your clothing onto the paper dolls.

1. Decide what pictures you are going to use with your paper dolls so you can decide how you want the dolls to look and what they should be wearing. Start simple; if you are fishing, have them wear fishing clothes and make a fishing pole.
2. Decorate the dolls. Make the clothes out of scraps of paper. Layer them for a realistic look. Add hair, eyes, and shoes. You can color these in or cut bits of paper to use. Glue the clothes onto your paper doll.
3. Time to accessorize. For a fishing doll, make a fishing pole and use a sticker for the fish. Look at what you have at home to add to the paper doll. Be creative and have fun.

Kid's Project #2—Put Dreams in Your Pocket Pages

This is a popular project, and you can find many inspiring ideas all around you. The concept is to create a paper pocket to go on your scrapbook page to hold items that you want to keep, such as report cards, letters, valentines, ticket stubs, and collector cards. You can keep all of these items in your scrapbook, and it is much easier to find the item when you need it.

You need the following supplies:

- Paper for pocket
- Paper for background page
- Stickers, die cuts, scraps of paper to decorate pocket
- Scissors
- Glue
- Pen

Here are the instructions:

1. Cut the paper for the pocket page in half the long way.
2. Put glue on three outside edges of the pocket and place on background paper.
3. Decorate your pocket any way you like.
4. Wait for glue to dry and gently place items inside pocket.

Following are some other ideas for pocket pages.

- Put a pocket in the middle of the page. Just glue the sides and stick letters down the middle.
- Use large die cuts to make your pocket into a shape, such as a bus or schoolhouse.
- You can make small pockets throughout the page to hold special tickets.

Kid's Project #3—Basketball, Bugs, or the Bassoon

My kids like to customize their books as much as possible. Let them decorate the cover using stickers and accents—if it doesn't stay on forever the world won't come to an end.

Decorated album. This personalized album is a great place for kids to store their scrapbook pages.

You need the following supplies:

◆ Glue

◆ Scissors

◆ Leftover stickers and accents

◆ Clear contact paper/laminating paper

Here are the instructions:

1. Decide what accents you want to use.
2. Place accents on binder.
3. Draw a title on a scrap of cardstock, place on binder.
4. Glue all pieces down.
5. Put laminating paper over the cover.

Journal

To encourage writing and creative thinking, have the kids create a paper journal for recording memories and events. You can purchase a notebook or have them make one with cardstock. Before they begin gather all of your necessary supplies in one area and let the kids go for it.

Include text in a variety of ways.

Parents and Kids Together

Children can be encouraged to join in the fun with Mom and Dad. Some innovative scrapbooking stores have realized that kids are interested in scrapbooking and are offering classes especially for them. Among the classes I have developed are a 12-week kids' summer camp, kids' basics, and kids' design. My latest is Baby-Sitting Mania, which features projects and games to add to a baby-sitting kit.

Try holding a scrapbooking party for kids. If your local scrapbook store has space, use their classroom. If not, you can throw one at home. Here's how:

- Pick a theme (summer, picnics, poolside, beach, or anything the kids might like) and ask each guest to bring some related pictures. That way, you can have a packet of appropriate die cuts and stickers for them. Let the kids experiment with scissors and punches.

- Relate the party games to scrapbooking— Pin the die cut on the page, scraptionery, sticker match game, and so on. When I play scraptionery with the kids, I have a bunch of cards with scrapbook items written down on them, such as decorative scissors, stationery, memorabilia pockets, and so forth. While you may not be able to come up with hundreds of items to draw, the kids will have fun playing this game. Give them a set amount of time and let them draw.

- As part of the fun, make an oversize scrapbook page to give to the birthday girl or boy. Ask each guest to bring a picture of themselves and have them glue it on the page and write what they like most about the birthday child.

- Favor bags would be a breeze to come up with—they could include die cuts, stickers, pens, cardstock, and much more.

Sticky Points

Some of the smaller scrapbook stores are not yet kid-friendly. If that describes your local store, try to encourage them to start classes for kids or offer workshops.

Kids learn best from hands-on experience. In the tool section of my kids' camp curricula, I show them how to use different tools and different ways to use them. In addition to showing kids the right way to use the tools, you can also teach the kids to sharpen their observation skills and their eyes for color and pattern. For instance, give each child a pair of scissors and ask them to find some paper that would match the pattern or show them all of the different ways to use punches other than just punching the shape out and gluing it on.

Photography Tips for Kids

As soon as kids start scrapbooking, they usually begin wanting to take their own photographs. I think you will be surprised at how much they love taking their own pictures. Here are some tips for getting children started taking their own pictures:

◆ Make sure they know to hold the camera steady until they have clicked the button.

◆ Cameras with an automatic focus and an automatic flash are generally easier for children to use, but if the camera is manual, show them how to advance the film so they can take the next shot.

◆ Teach them to take the pictures at their level or to climb up (safely!) or crouch down if they are taking photos of objects higher or lower than they are.

◆ Instruct them on how to get everything in the picture by looking through the camera's viewfinder and making sure the things they want to take photos of are within the viewfinder's lines.

◆ Tell them to take their time and compose the shots—they don't need to rush.

Shortcuts _____

If you aren't sure whether to buy a camera for your child, try purchasing a disposable camera to see how interested they really are.

Let them enjoy taking the pictures and putting them in their scrapbook. This would be a great summer project.

Safety First

While having fun with the kids, don't forget to take precautions, especially because the children will be using scissors and other cutting tools. Show kids exactly how to use tools that they may not be familiar with and go over safety rules when you begin any project.

Safe Cutting

Remind children that scissors are meant to cut paper, not hair, clothes, or skin. Though decorative scissors don't have very sharp blades, you can still do some damage with them, so remind kids to handle them properly. The same goes for paper trimmers and die cuts, which have sharp blades. It would be best for an adult to closely supervise when kids use either of these cutting tools.

Sticky Points

Keep safety in mind when working with kids. Here are some safety tips for working with kids:

◆ Use scissors the safe way (children should hold a closed pair of scissors by the blade, and, of course, should never run with them).

◆ Check out one tool at a time to avoid clutter.

◆ Create a safety cutting zone for paper cutters.

◆ Adult supervision is suggested with die-cut machines.

Keep a Neat and Organized Work Area

As with any craft project, it is important to keep your area picked up so you and the kids won't trip over the punch that fell to the floor or step on that pair of scissors. I let my kids choose one tool at a time to use, and they have to trade that tool in before they can get another one. Designate spots for tools and train kids to use tools and put them back in the right place. The work area will be neater and safer.

The Least You Need to Know

◆ You and your child will have fun together trying some of the projects in this chapter.

◆ Be patient and teach children the skills—let them create without your interference or "help."

◆ Encourage children to write down their thoughts in their own handwriting.

◆ Ask your local scrapbooking store to offer classes and projects for kids.

◆ Remind kids to use tools and materials safely.

In This Part

Part 6

Post-Grad Scrapping

No matter how many scrapbookers I meet and talk to, they all have one thing in common: They want ideas, ideas, and more ideas. Scrapbookers love to use the latest crafting techniques to make their albums more meaningful. In these next four chapters, you will get ideas on how to use all the mixed media, and how to incorporate traditional crafting techniques into your scrapbooking. To best illustrate the variety of uses, I turned to the experts on the design team at www.scrapjazz.com to contribute their layouts.

In This Chapter

◆ Different ways to adhere trims in your scrapbook

◆ Suggested uses for craft wire

◆ What fibers are, where to get them, and how to use them

Terrific Trims

Being a mom of all boys, I haven't had much use for all the ribbons and trims I see at the craft and fabric stores. Until now! I am so pleased that I can put these in my scrapbooks. I do suggest that you treat any trims that you buy with a deacidifying spray, to lower the possibility that they will harm your photos.

You can find trim at your fabric stores, craft stores, scrapbooking stores, quilting stores, and more!

Ribbon

Ginghams, floral, wired, sheer—these are just a few of the types of ribbon that are available. Try using ribbon to create a simple border or frame. You can also "write" with it and create a fun title or caption. Because ribbon is available in many different widths (from $\frac{1}{16}$ an inch to 3 or 4 inches), you're sure to find just the right size for your page.

Check out these online sites to purchase some ribbon:

www.ribbonshop.com

www.theprintersdaughter.com (sold by the yard)

www.scrapbookluv.com (sold by the yard)

www.scrapbooking.com (other ideas on using ribbon)

I love using a spray adhesive to mount my ribbon to my pages. It covers the ribbon evenly and thinly, and you don't get the messy overflow that you can get with glues. Plus, if you're using a sheer ribbon, the spray adhesive won't show through. Other adhesives you can try are Xyron or glue dots.

(Layout by Lynn McCory, scrapjazz.com)

Here the ribbon is used to create a simple border.

I created an elegant-looking bulletin board–style page using ribbon.

(Layout by Andrea Steed, scrapjazz.com)

Notice the use of ribbon as trim on the knife.

Sticky Points

When working with ribbon or fabric, you'll often find that your adhesive will get stuck on the front of the ribbon somehow. A baby wipe works wonders—just wipe the adhesive off and let dry.

Wicked Wire

I can recall when metallic paper first became available to use in scrapbooks and people went crazy over it. I was bemused, because it didn't appeal to me at all. Then I tried it and loved it! You can get a bright, shiny, bold look with metal.

That metal look has carried over into trims! Scrapbookers all over are using craft wire in their albums. It is available in a variety of colors and widths. The smaller the gauge, the thicker the wire. There are even special tools to help you create any masterpiece you can dream up. I have seen it used to create braces for a million-dollar-smile layout, a barbed wire fence, and even bugs. You will soon find a favorite use for it and will want to keep it on hand as a scrapbooking staple.

The easiest way to affix wire to your layout is to poke holes in your paper and hook it behind the paper, dabbing the end with a bit of glue. If that doesn't work then try using the tiny glue dots, or your favorite spray adhesive.

(Layout by Tammy Jackson, scrapjazz.com)

The bugs are created out of wire.

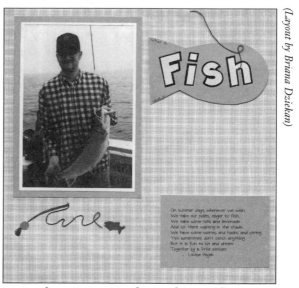

(Layout by Briana Dziekan)

Here the wire is used to enhance the accent.

(Layout by Tammy Jackson, scrapjazz.com)

The use of wire ties the photos to the page.

Go here to get some wire for your supply box:

www.scrapbookemporium.com
www.artisticwire.com (ideas on using wire)
www.gonescrappin.com

Shortcuts _____

Like the look of wire but don't want to take the time to twist it yourself? Purchase pre-formed wire accents. They come in a variety of designs. Just check your local craft store.

Fibers

Fibers entered the scrapbooking world with a bang. We first saw them in a publication by Becky Higgins, *Scrapbooking Secrets*, used in scrapbooking. The uses are as endless as the selection. See the accompanying figures for some of my favorite uses.

Words for Posterity _____

Fibers refers to a specific type of decorative yarn found at quilting and embroidery stores.

(Layout by Lynn McCory, scrapjazz.com)

The fiber wrapped around the photo mount is beautiful.

(Layout by Robyn Ricks, scrapjazz.com)

The fibers used as a simple accent highlight the simplicity of the layout.

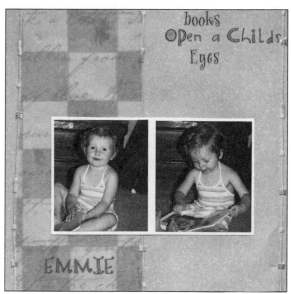

Let the design of the fiber help dictate its placement on the layout, as in the layout shown here.

There are a few ways to adhere fibers to your page, depending on what you're doing and how you're using the fibers. When placing fibers directly on a page I like to use glue dots. If I am adhering fibers to an accent that will later be placed on the page, then I like to use memory mount glue or spray adhesive. You can also punch holes in the page, string it through the holes, and glue on the back of the page. Experiment and see which way you like best.

Shortcuts

Join a fiber swap to get your fiber collection started. Fiber swaps are a great inexpensive way to experiment with the different fibers so you can invest your dollars in the fibers you like best.

Look at these places for a great selection of fibers:

www.funkyfibers.com (devoted to fibers)

www.thecardladies.com (huge selection)

www.stamperstouch.com (card-making ideas)

From the Archives

Fibers were first used in the rubber stamping world. It didn't take too long for scrapbookers to fall in love with them as well.

Other Trims

Next time you're shopping in your favorite fabric store or craft store, look around at all of the trims, from ric rac to lace, and think of all the scrapbooking possibilities. Imagine lace on a wedding layout, or ric rac on that class picture of you from the 1970s. You can pick up trim ideas everywhere. I find mine in the most unusual places and enjoy experimenting with different textures.

To get the look of wire without the fuss, try using pre-made wire titles such as this one.

(Layout by Andrea Steed, scrapjazz.com)

These things do I love:
Old things, old places,
Remembered things, familiar faces.

The simple combination of wire and fibers works well.

A simple yet fancy trim combo!

Check out these websites for some fabulous ideas on using trim in your scrapbooks:

www.croppincorner.com

www.impressrubberstamps.com

www.gonescrappin.com

Shortcuts

Wrap your leftover trim around your cardstock scraps to prevent it from becoming creased or bent. Store in a plastic shoebox and you're set to go.

The Least You Need to Know

◆ One adhesive that will work on all trims is glue dots.

◆ Try combining different types of trim for an interesting layout.

◆ Use elements from your photos to decide what type of trim to use.

◆ Refer to the websites listed in this chapter for the latest type of trim available for your scrapbook.

In This Chapter

◆ What kind of fasteners are popular in scrapbooking right now

◆ Stitch or glue buttons onto your pages to add dimension

◆ How to use eyelets to attach items to your page

Chapter 22

Fantastic Fasteners

How did they do that? I say this to myself frequently when perusing through published layouts, and I've discovered that many scrapbookers use a variety of ways to fasten accents, photo mats, and trim to their layout. In this chapter, you will find out about a variety of these methods as I take you through the most popular.

Brads

Long a staple of kids' arts and crafts projects, *brads* are making their way onto scrapbook pages. But they've undergone a transformation. While you'll still be able to find the traditional brass-colored brads, they are now available in myriad colors. Pastel green, bright pink, muted orange, you name it, it's out there! And they're available in a variety of sizes, too: oversize, and my favorite, mini brads.

Brads are simple to use! I use them to connect elements to my pages, incorporate them into my journaling, fasten tags to pages with them, and so on. Rather than use the brad's prongs to pierce the page, I find it's easiest to punch a hole with my hole punch, and then place the brad through the holes.

Words for Posterity

Brads are a longtime office supply staple used to fasten pages together or adhere items to a page. A brad resembles a thumbtack with a decorative head and two prongs for a stem. To use it you puncture your pages with the prongs and secure the pages together by spreading the prongs apart.

(Layout by Gayla Feachen)

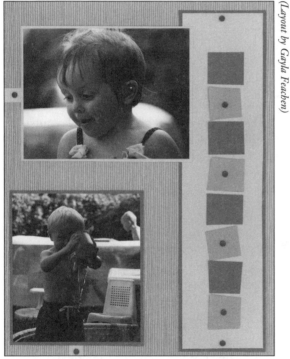

This layout uses brads to hold the vellum in place.

Look how the brads hold the tags in place.

Brads come in all colors and shapes. These star brads are a perfect accent.

Of course you can buy the standard brads at any office supply store, but for other sizes you'll need to look to your local scrapbook specialty store. Or check out some of these online stores:

www.scrappinfools.com

www.memoriesoftherabbit.com

www.houseofscraps.com

Sticky Points

To save time when working with cardstock, use a paper piercer to make your hole instead of the brad's prongs.

Buttons

One of the first sewing skills I learned in home economics was sewing on buttons. I thought it was so much fun that I kept practicing on anything I could find: scraps, doll clothes, even washcloths. Now I am rediscovering the fun of buttons in my scrapbooks! Only now, sewing is optional. I like to use buttons as accents on my pages, as they can add depth to the layout.

There are a couple ways to adhere buttons to your pages. You can go with the traditional sewing method and "stitch" the buttons to your page using matching fiber or embroidery floss. Or you can use an adhesive like memory mount glue. I also like to use glue dots, because they are simple to work with and provide a very firm hold!

(Layout by Jenny Benge, scrapjazz.com)

I enjoy seeing how other designers I like use buttons as they tend to suggest more of a country look. I love how Jenny Benge has used them on this charming layout.

(Layout by Beth Batt, scrapjazz.com)

Grouping buttons of different sizes and colors works well as an accent as seen in this layout.

Buttons are used to accent and add dimension and interest to this page.

You can find buttons anywhere! Check out your local fabric store and your scrapbook store. Don't overlook places like garage sales and thrift shops. You might find a shirt or dress with great buttons that you can cut off. And don't forget to ask Grandma for her button collection to see if you can find that perfect old-fashioned button.

Check out these sites for more buttons:

www.gonescrappin.com

www.memories.com

www.myscrapbooklane.com

Shortcuts

If you're in need of some unique buttons check your local thrift shop for old clothes with interesting buttons. This method tends to be less expensive than buying the actual buttons.

Eyelets

Think grommets on a miniature scale. *Eyelets* are a fabulous addition to your pages. You can use them to attach vellum, to string fibers through, or to accent. Eyelets are available in all sorts of styles and sizes.

Words for Posterity

An **eyelet** is a small metal ring with a hole in the center through which fibers or other material can be threaded. The eyelet also helps to reinforce the hole in the page. Because it separates into two halves, it can also be used as a decorative fastener and accent in its own right.

To work with eyelets you need a setter. After you have made the hole for the eyelet, you insert the eyelet, turn over the page, and pound the eyelet flat with your setter. This technique is easy to master in no time at all.

From the Archives

The eyelet or grommet was commonly used in sewing and home decorating. When industry expert Becky Higgins debuted her *Scrapbooking Secrets* idea book in 2000, she introduced everyone to the world of eyelets as she artistically used them throughout her best-selling book.

(Layout by Jenny Benge, scrapjazz.com)

Using eyelets is one of the biggest trends in scrapbooking.

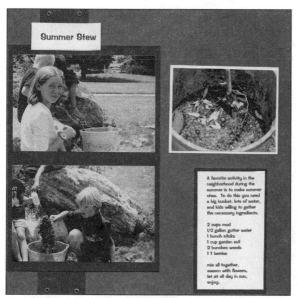

This page was a breeze to complete with easy fasteners.

The eyelets hold the journaling in place.

For a good selection of eyelets shop here:

www.scrapbook-warehouse.com

www.scrapbugs.com

www.scrapbookutopia.com

Other Fasteners

Even if you're not big on hanging your clothes on a clothesline you'll love mini clothespins on your pages. They are available in a huge variety of colors and patterns. Try using other fasteners you find as well such as jump rings used to make jewelry. See the following figures for inspiration.

Here the clothespins hold the accents on the page.

Nail heads look just like brads and come in a variety of styles.

(Layout by Marpy Hayse, scrapjazz.com)

The jump rings are holding the fibers together in the middle.

These circular paper clips are all the rage; they are both practical and decorative.

Browse through the virtual aisles of these online stores for more fasteners:

www.twopeasinabucket.com

www.scrapnstuff.com

www.scrappingbyalaine.com

 Shortcuts

Use fasteners to attach vellum when you don't want the adhesive to show.

The Least You Need to Know

◆ Access scrapbooking.com to read their article about creative uses for brads.

◆ Fasteners are perfect for affixing accents to your page.

◆ Pick up a variety of fasteners at your local office supply store.

In This Chapter

◆ Oodles of unique ideas for accents that will give your pages flair

◆ The answer to "How on earth did you get that to stay on your page?"

◆ How to add sparkle to your glitzy photos

Chapter 23

Awesome Accents

Accents carry your page to success. Start using accents and you'll find yourself walking the aisles of your craft store in a whole new way! Every item holds possibilities for your pages. Each bauble or bead could be the perfect item to tell your photo story.

Accents will really bring out your creativity, plus they are affordable and fun to work with.

Beads

Who among us didn't love stringing beads as a child? Remember that macaroni necklace you made for your aunt's birthday? Well, you can use beads in your scrapbook and recapture the fun you had as a child. Beads add instant pizzazz to your pages, and they are available in endless varieties.

Try stringing the beads on your trim, or using glue dots to apply them directly to your page. If beading is something you will use extensively, it's a good idea to buy special beading tools, like pliers and sorting trays.

You will find what you're looking for here:

www.scrappatch.com
www.scrapoodles.com
www.memories.com

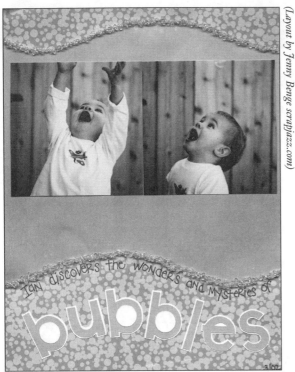

(Layout by Jenny Benge scrapjazz.com)

Note how the beads are used as a border.

Here the beads are strung as an accent.

The beads add a playful nature to this layout.

Shortcuts

Purchase storage containers for your beads, as they easily get mixed up.

All That Glitters

For the inner beauty queen in all of us, here are some fun ways to add shimmer to your layouts. Try glitter, jewels, or mirrors. They are simple to use, but can be used in many different ways, making them a perfect medium to work with!

Try using glitter for your titles, adding mirrors to those little girl dress-up pages, or using jewels on the layout with photos of you on the Pirates of the Caribbean ride!

The best way to adhere glitter and tinsel is to follow the manufacturer suggestions. My favorite technique is to use the sticky tacky tape sold at craft stores. Lay the tape down, pour your glitter over it, and then shake off the extra glitter. Stick the other side to your layout, and there you have it! For jewels and mirrors, try glue dots or memory mount glue.

Here are some sites you can go to for these types of accents:

www.magicscraps.com

www.jewelcraftbiz.com (ideas)

www.thescrapbox.com

Shortcuts

Glue your glitter accents onto your page last so the glitter won't fall off on your photos.

The jewels work well to highlight the feminine side of this layout.

Metal Accents

Don't overlook metal when putting your albums together. It can add a classic touch to any page. Charms in hundreds of styles abound and can be found to match any theme. I enjoy looking at my craft store for different metal accessories.

The glitter works well as a title here and complementary accent.

Won't the viewers of your album be surprised when they look at this page!

When adhering these items I have had the most success with glue dots. Just place them on the layout and then place the metal pieces on top. If this doesn't hold then try to use a tacky glue such as Memory Mount. Be sure to let dry overnight.

These sports charms highlight the child's interests.

Look at these websites to purchase your metal accents:

www.twopeasinabucket.com (great selection of charms)

www.magicscraps.com

www.dmarie.com

From the Archives _____

Magic Scraps is a newly formed company devoted to unique accents. They recently introduced a tool for inscribing on metal and blank metal tags.

This unique accent of tin stars gives this page that Americana look.

Other Accents

From miniature watch faces to clear glass *picture pebbles*, you will find an amazing assortment of accents in today's scrapbooks. How can you keep up on all the latest accents? The best way is to subscribe to your favorite scrapbook store's mailing list, keep your magazine subscriptions current, and attend conventions. Conventions are where you will see all the newest items being used.

Words for Posterity _____

Picture pebbles are smooth, flat, clear-colored pebbles. Use these to place over words to give them an enlarged or distorted look.

Go to your local craft store and look down every aisle. Try your home improvement store, too. I have seen chicken wire and all sorts of nuts and bolts being used in scrapbooking. Following are some layouts with my favorite miscellaneous accents.

The picture pebbles enlarge the words.

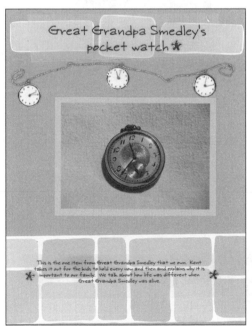

Here the miniature watch face captures the mood of the layout.

(Layout by Stephanie Bryson)

The cutest little place to put your accents— a bitty bag.

Words for Posterity

A **bitty bag** is a small bag made from translucent fabric that is perfect to attach to your page with a trinket inside.

These websites have great ideas for other types of accents:

www.addictedtoscrapbooks.com

www.scrapadoodledoo.com

www.thescrapbox.com

The Least You Need to Know

◆ Don't forget to save those charms to add to your scrapbook page.

◆ Add meaning to your journaling by using picture pebbles to highlight specific words.

◆ Check out this website for more ideas on adding accents to your page: www. twopeasinabucket.com.

In This Chapter

- ◆ Use everything in your craft closet for enhancing your scrapbooks, from sewing items to rubber-stamping supplies

- ◆ How to dry emboss to give your page that discreet dimension

- ◆ What accents you can create with all of those paper scraps

Chapter 24

Time-Tested Techniques

When attending trade conventions it's easy to become overwhelmed by the hundreds of booths showcasing all of the latest items available in the crafting world. It can be daunting when learning all there is to know about basic scrapbooking. When you're ready for more you'll find a wealth of information available for you. In this chapter, I'll touch on a few craft techniques that have crossed over into scrapbooking to become standard technique.

Stitching and Sewing

Whether you do it by machine or by hand, stitching and sewing is a favorite among scrapbookers. You can add a homespun feel to your pages and create interesting titles and photo mounts using these techniques.

Stitching

Regardless of how you use stitching on your pages, here are some basic instructions:

◆ You need a needle and thread to start. Try cross-stitch needles—they work well with the heavier weight cardstock.

◆ Try embroidery floss for thread, because you can make it as thick as you need.

◆ When stitching directly on your page, remember that it doesn't have to be perfect; you want it to look handmade.

- If you don't want to use a needle, try a paper piercer.
- For variety, use ribbon, raffia, tinsel, hemp, yarn, and fibers to sew in your book.

(Layout by Andrea Steed scrapjazz.com)

Here the hand stitching highlights the title.

Sewing

Because so many scrapbookers dabble in other crafts as well, it didn't take long for machine sewing on pages to appear. It's a great way to add subtle texture to your page without overwhelming your photos. Many scrapbookers love to create random patterns by sewing scraps onto the background paper and then mounting photos on top. Try sewing paper to create pockets for keepsakes. Whatever you decide to sew on you will enjoy the look this technique adds.

Here are some instructions:

- Load appropriate needle in machine.
- Temporarily hold together paper that is going to be sewn together.
- Insert paper in machine and tread slowly.
- When turning, reposition paper before you turn to avoid tearing the paper.
- At the end, clip thread and dab a bit of glue to keep it from unraveling.

(Layout by Jenny Benge scrapjazz.com)

The scraps are sewn directly on the layout with a machine.

Dry Embossing

Dry embossing is a lovely look that card makers have been using for years. When you dry emboss you create a raised impression on the paper that makes it appear to stand out. By using simple tools you can accomplish this with just about any type of paper and any type of template. Try using this technique on your wedding pages for a subtle yet beautiful way to accent your layout.

Words for Posterity

Dry embossing is done when you create an impression on paper using a blunt tool.

Here are some simple instructions:

◆ You need a stylus, template or stencil, light box, and paper (thick works better).

◆ Secure stencil or template on top of light box.

◆ Place paper on top of stencil, secure into place.

◆ Trace design with stylus tool, slowly to avoid tearing.

◆ Add color to the raised design if desired.

Go to these sites for more ideas:

www.more-than-memories.com

www.liforpaper.com

www.brassstencils.com

Shortcuts

Try sticking your pattern up to the window, placing your paper over the pattern, then rolling away with your embosser.

(Layout by Lynn McCory scrapjazz.com)

The accents on this layout are dry embossed to give a 3-D feel to the layout.

The background strip is embossed and then chalked.

Quilling

Quilling is an art that has been around since Renaissance times. It is the art of rolling thin strips of paper into coils to create decorative items such as flowers. This is a fun craft to learn, as you need only a few basic tools and your imagination.

Words for Posterity

Quilling is the art of rolling paper strips into different formations such as flowers and shapes.

Here are some basic instructions:

♦ You need thin strips of paper from $\frac{1}{8}$ inch to 1 inch.

♦ Glue for gluing ends of project.

♦ Something to construct paper coil around such as a toothpick, crochet hook, pencil, or anything else that will work with your desired shape.

♦ After you have your supplies start quilling paper into desired coil shape.

♦ To maintain shape dab a bit of glue on the ends and let sit overnight.

To find out more about this historical crafting go to the following websites:

www.handcraftersvillage.com/quilling.htm

www.quilling.com

www.creatingkeepsakes.com

(Layout by Lynn McCory scrapjazz.com)

Flowers with centers quilled.

The quilling on this friendship page is simple and playful.

Stamping

Stamping has been around much longer than scrapbooking and has continued to inspire scrapbookers to try out new techniques. Rubber stamping involves the transferring of a design onto a flat surface such as paper, using ink. After you have chosen your stamp then you ink it and go. Beyond that there are a million and one things you can do with your rubber stamps, from decorating your room to creating artful collages for wall décor.

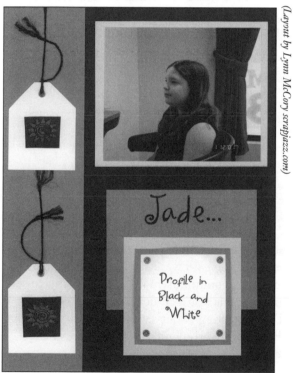

*(Layout by **Lynn McCory** scrapjazz.com)*

Stamping in tags.

Try stamping on your background paper to create a pattern as done in this layout.

Shortcuts

Use baby wipes to clean the ink off your stamps before you put them away. Taking good care of stamps increases their life span.

Check out these sites for more on stamping:

www.rubberstampinglinks.com

www.heroarts.com

www.limitededitionrs.com

Paper Piecing

All you need to *paper piece* is the ability to trace, cut, and paste. To achieve a variety of looks you can paper piece just about anything. You can purchase patterns from a variety of places or create your own.

> **Words for Posterity**
>
> **Paper piecing** is tracing pattern pieces on paper, cutting the pieces out, then assembling the pieces to create a picture.

Here are some basic instructions:

- Start with all supplies on hand for this project—pattern, pencil, scissors, adhesive.
- Trace the pattern onto pieces of paper. To avoid tracing lines, use a tracing pencil—one that will let you erase on any type of paper and won't discolor the paper.
- Cut out the pieces you've traced.
- Adhere the pieces together starting with big pieces first and putting smaller ones on top.
- Embellish with chalks, markers, or accents to give it the desired look.

If you love paper piecing and are looking for new designs, try www.scrapola.com. They will deliver new designs to you each month or you can request to have custom designs made for you.

Here is a piece done by Scrapola designer Melissa Cleverly. The patterns for the frog, hair, eyes, and so on were traced and cut out separately, then glued together.

Serendipity Squares

serendipity: n. accidental sagacity; the faculty of making fortunate discoveries of things you were not looking for.

As with several other hot trends in scrapbooking (fibers being a good example), *serendipity squares* were started by the rubberstamping community. We are beginning to see more of this hot technique in scrapbooking. The best thing about serendipity squares is that they are fail-proof and fun to make using scraps.

Words for Posterity

Serendipity squares are small collage pieces that have been created by randomly gluing scraps on a large sheet of paper, then cutting the large collage piece into squares.

Here are instructions for making basic squares:

- Start with a large rectangle of solid colored scrap.
- Randomly stamp on the background using one or two designs.
- Adhere scraps of pattern paper, cardstock, or any other textured type of paper.
- Add any accents you may want such as fibers, stickers, or punches.
- Cut into uniform squares and adhere onto your page.

You will enjoy this crafting process and the result as well. Remember, the look is that of collage and is meant to be random—you can control the color and the properties, but not the result. Enjoy!

For more techniques and info go to these sites:

www.gracefulbee.com

www.stampsinksiteme.com

www.gotastamp.com

(Layout by Marpy Hayse scrapjazz.com)

Serendipity squares. The colors work well on this layout with the focus being on the photos.

The Least You Need to Know

- Use your stamps to create page accents and background to enhance your layouts.
- When creating serendipity squares remember there are no rules.
- Create paper-pieced accents for your pages using patterns made especially for scrapbookers.
- Watch general crafting trends for new techniques to use in your scrapbooking.

Resource Guide

The following companies, organizations, and websites offer scrapbookers products and information.

Products

Following is a sampling of some of my favorite products.

Archival Mist
preservation spray
www.ptlp.com/a_index.html

Artistic Wire
wire and tools
www.artisticwire.com

Close to My Heart
stamps
www.closetomyheart.com

Cock a Doodle Design
pre-illustrated pieces, consultant program
www.cockadoodledesign.com

C-Line Products, Inc.
protectors
www.c-lineproducts.com/MemoryBook

Crop in Style
storage products
www.cropinstyle.com

Dalee Book Company
albums
www.daleebook.com

EK Success, Ltd.
a little bit of everything
www.eksucess.com

Family Treasures
punches, storage, and more
www.familytreasures.com

Fiskars
scissors, punches, and more
www.fiskars.com

Funky Fibers
fibers kits, scraps
www.funkyfibers.com

Generations
storage products
www.generationsnow.com

Glue Dots International
adhesive
www.gluedots.com

Graffitti Stickers
title stickers
www.scrapbookborders.com/graffiti.html

Hero Arts
rubber stamps
www.heroarts.com

Honey Tree
paper, stickers
www.thehoney-tree.com

Jewelcraft
beads and accessories
www.jewelcraft.biz

K&Company
paper, albums
www.kandcompany.com

KI Memories, Inc.
Cutting Edge Designs
www.cuttingedge-designs.com

Manco, Inc.
adhesives
www.duckproducts.com

Me and My Big Ideas Stickers
stickers and paper
www.meandmybigideas.com

My Mind's Eye
pre-illustrated products
www.frame-ups.com

Paper Adventures
paper, stickers, and more
www.paperadventures.com

Paper Reflections
paper, albums
www.dmdind.com

Paper Patch
patterned paper
www.paperpatch.com

Photosaver
photo cleaning clothes
www.photosavercloth.com

Pioneer Photo Albums®
albums
www.pioneerphotoalbums.com

PuzzleMates
templates
www.puzzlemates.com

SEI
stickers and paper
www.shopsei.com

Magazines

Craftworks Home and Garden
www.craftsworkmag.com

Creating Keepsakes
1-888-247-5282 (subscriptions)
www.creatingkeepsakes.com

Family Tree Magazine
www.familytreemagazine.com

Ivy Cottage Creations Magazine
1-888-303-1375 (subscriptions)
www.ivycottagecreations.com

Memory Makers Magazine
www.memorymakersmagazine.com

PaperKuts Scrapbook Magazine
1-888-881-5861 (subscriptions)
www.paperkuts.com

Scrapbooks, Etc.
newsstand six times a year

Simple Scrapbook Magazine
866-334-8149 (subscriptions)
www.simplescrapbookmag.com

Websites

www.croppingcentral.com

www.croppingqueens.com

www.jangle.com

www.gracefulbee.com

www.gonescrappin.com

www.rubberstampinglinks.com

www.scrapbooking.com

www.scrapbookarticles.com

www.scrapbooksites.com

www.scrapjazz.com

www.scrappinfools.com

www.twopeasinabucket.com

Retreats/Conventions

Camp Crop
luxurious retreat
www.campcrop.com

Crazed Cropper
weekend getaway for the scrapbooker
www.crazedcropper.com

Dream Events
traveling crops
www.dreameventsinc.com

Great American Scrapbook Convention
consumer show
www.greatamericanscrapbook.com

Magical Memory Adventures
weekend getaway
www.magicalmemoryadventures.com

Memories Expo
consumer convention
www.memoriesexpo.com

Scrapbook Expo
consumer convention
www.scrapbookexpo.com

Scrapbook Tour
traveling crop
www.scrapbooktour.com

Appendix B

Suggested Reading

Auth, Betty. *Stamping Tricks for Scrapbooks: A Guide for Enhancing Your Pages with Stamps.* Gloucester, MA: Rockport Publishers, 2002.

Beachum, Alison, and Helen Naylor. *Buttons, Bows, Strings, and Things.* San Diego, CA: Pine Cone Press, 2002.

Bearnson, Lisa. *Mom's Little Book of Displaying Children's Art.* Bluffdale, UT: Porch Swing Publishing, 2001.

———. *Mom's Little Book of Photo Tips.* Bluffdale, UT: Porch Swing Publishing, 2001.

Crowe, Elizabeth Powell. *Genealogy Online.* Colombus, OH: Osborne McGraw-Hill, 2001.

Daly, Tim. *The Desktop Photographer: How to Make Great Photographs with Your Computer.* New York, NY: Watson-Guptill Publications, 2002.

Editorial team, Krause Publications. *Kids 1st Scrapbooking.* Iola, WI: Krause Publications, 2002.

Higgins, Becky. *My Creative Companion.* Bluffdale, UT: Porch Swing Publishing, 2001.

Johnson, Robin. *Designing with Vellum.* Encino, CA: Autumn Leaves.

Johnson, Robin, Debbie Crouse, and Heidi Swapp. *Designing with Notions.* Encino, CA: Autumn Leaves, 2002.

Julian, Stacy. *Simple Scrapbooks.* Bluffdale, UT: Porch Swing Publishing, 2001.

Kirschner, Bev Braun. *New Ideas for Crafting Heritage Albums.* Betterway Pubns, 2001.

Krause, Jim. *Color Index: Over 11,000 Color Combinations, CMYK and RGB Formulas, for Print and Web Media.* Cincinatti, OH: How Design Books, 2002.

McClure, Rhonda. *The Official Family Tree Maker Fast and Easy Version 9.* Cambridge, MA: Premier Press, 2001.

Pederson, Angie. *The Book of Me: A Guide to Scrapbooking About Yourself.* Cincinatti, OH: Efg, Inc., 2002.

Redburn, Sandy. *500 Great Heartwarming Expressions for Scrapbooking and Cards.* Surrey, Canada: Crafty Secrets Publications, 2001.

Slan, Joanna Campbell. *One Minute Journaling.* Cincinatti, OH: Efg, Inc., 2001.

Taylor, Maureen. *Preserving Your Family Photographs: How to Organize, Present, and Restore Your Precious Family Images.* Betterway Pubns, 2001.

Taylor, Stephanie. *Family Scrapbooking.* New York, NY: Sterling Publishing, 2001.

Words for Posterity

acid   A substance that fades photographs. Found in most paper.

adhesive   Any substance used to make items stick to each other (for example, glue, paste, tape, or reversible adhesives).

album   Blank book used to store photographs and scrapbook pages.

analogous colors   Colors that are next to each other on the color wheel.

aperture   The opening in a camera that lets in light. The aperture opens and closes when the shutter is released.

archival   Term used to describe a product or technique used in preserving artifacts, photos, memorabilia, and other items.

basic templates   Templates in basic shapes (ovals, circles, and so on).

bitty bag   A small bag made from translucent fabric that is perfect to attach to your page with a trinket inside.

blending pencil   Tool used to blend colored pencils to create shades of a color.

bold colors   Bright, high-intensity colors.

brads   A longtime office supply staple. Used to puncture paper and adhere together by spreading apart the two prongs.

buffered   Term used to describe products capable of maintaining the basicity of a solution. Buffered paper prevents acid from moving from a photo to paper.

calligraphy   Formal, old-fashioned lettering.

calligraphy pen   Pen with a slanted tip designed to write calligraphy.

cardstock   Thick, sturdy paper available in a variety of weights.

CASE   An online abbreviation meaning Copy And Steal Everything. If you CASE a layout you duplicate the page or project.

CK OK   Creating Keepsakes Okay. Scrap-booking seal of approval; items that have the CK OK designation are considered safe to use in scrapbooks.

clip art   Art purchased in book or software form with pictures that can be applied to scrapbook pages.

collage   An artistic composition made of various materials (such as paper, cloth, or wood) and glued onto a surface.

color wheel   Shows color relationships and placement.

complementary colors   Colors that are opposite each other on a color wheel.

conservationist   Someone who studies archival methods and techniques and uses them to preserve artifacts, artworks, or precious documents.

corner-edger scissors   Scissors that cut corners. Each pair creates four different types of corners.

corrugated paper   Thick, wavy cardstock available in many colors.

crop   (1) To cut or trim a photo. (2) A scrapbooking party hosted by an expert who shares techniques, products, and information with the group.

cutouts   Designs that are meant to be cut out. They don't have perforated edges.

deacidification spray   Spray that neutralizes acid in newspaper clippings, certificates, and other documents.

decorative scissors   Scissors with a decorative pattern on the blade.

die-cut designs   Paper designs cut from die-cut machines. Paper is placed on the die and pressure is applied either by rolling or pressing down on the handle.

double-mount   To place a photo on two background papers.

dry embossing   When a you create an impression on paper using a blunt tool.

embellishments   Any scrapbooking extras, such as stickers, die cuts, and punches that enhance scrapbooking pages.

emboss   To create a raised surface by applying heat or pressure.

encapsulation   A method of displaying three-dimensional memorabilia and protecting nearby items from acid contained in the memorabilia. Items are encased in stable plastics.

eyelet   A two-part metal piece with a hole in the middle created to attach items together leaving the hole in the middle.

favorites file   A personal book of ideas and layouts.

fibers   Refers to a type of yarn that is decorative.

film speed   Refers to a film's sensitivity to light. Lower-speed films are less sensitive; use these on bright, sunny days. Higher-speed films are more sensitive; use these in low-light situations.

fine and chisel pen   This pen has a fine tip (0.5 mm) and a chisel tip (6.0 mm). The fine tip is good for lettering, and the chisel tip is very versatile.

fine-tip point pens   Pens with extremely small tips good for doodling and precise lettering. Pens tips range from .005 mm to .08 mm. Good for journaling and lettering.

focal point   The element of a design where lines converge. The eye is naturally drawn to the focal point in an image.

gel-based rollers   Pens with pigment ink.

genealogy   The study of the descent of a person, family, or group from an ancestor. Many people who wish to create a family tree start by researching their family's genealogy.

general pattern paper   Paper with patterns, such as stripes, dots, or plaids, that is made to be used for any occasion.

gift album   A compilation of photos and mementos created with a person or event in mind.

handmade paper   Paper made by hand that is often rough and uneven in texture. There are sometimes flowers or leaves in the paper, which add to the natural look.

handmade scraps   Embellishments made from layered-looking die cuts.

heading   The caption or title that explains the theme of a layout.

heritage   Traditions passed down from generation to generation.

idea books   Books usually about one aspect of scrapbooking. Some are written for particular themes, such as wedding, baby, or pets, while others are devoted to a particular product, like stickers, die cuts, or templates.

intensity   The strength of a color based on how true it is to the primary color.

journaling   Any words you write in your book, from titles and captions to long descriptions, poems, or stories.

journaling templates   Templates with space left for writing.

layout   The grouping of pages in your scrapbook that go together. Some layouts fit on one page, most fit on two, and some are put on panoramic layouts.

letter templates   Templates in the shape of letters of the alphabet.

light refraction   Light bent through a prism that shows the colors of the visible light spectrum: red, orange, yellow, green, blue, indigo, and violet.

lignin   A naturally occurring acid substance in wood that breaks down over time. Paper with lignin is not suitable for archival projects.

mass-merchandising store   Stores that sell a large variety of products from sundries to automotive tools to craft supplies.

master family album   Holds pictures of everyone in the family and family documents, typically in chronological order.

memorabilia   Certificates, documents, and other items that tell a story. Memorabilia can include souvenirs from trips and mementos from special occasions or historical events.

monochromatic color scheme   Employs different values of the same color.

mount   To adhere a photo, embellishment, or other item to another piece of paper.

muted colors   Subdued tints or shades of colors that tend to be more suitable for backgrounds.

oval croppers   Paper trimmers that cut paper and photographs into ovals.

page exchange   Participants are invited to create a page to share with other scrapbookers. Often, a theme is given, such as Halloween. Each participant brings enough copies of an original page to trade with the others.

page protectors   Plastic sheets that display and protect pages.

page toppers   Hand-drawn illustrated phrases in bright colors meant to be used as titles at the top of pages.

paint pens   Pens with soft, brush-like tips. The amount of ink dispensed is controlled by the pressure that is applied to the tip.

paper piecing   Tracing pattern pieces on paper, cutting these pieces out, then gluing all together to create an accent.

paper trimmers   Paper-cutting tools used by placing paper, lining it up on a grid, and moving down a blade.

pass the chocolate   A phrase commonly spoken by members of a scrapbooking club.

pattern paper   Paper with designs repeated on the entire page.

perforated punches   Shapes that the scrapbooker can use as embellishments on a page by punching out on the perforations.

pH level   Measurement that tells a scrapbooker how acidic or basic something is. For scrapbooking, you want to use products with a pH level of seven or above.

pH testing pen   Used to test the acidity of paper. The pen mark changes colors, depending on the level of acid present.

Photo Activity Test (P.A.T.)   This test, created by the American National Standards Institute, determines if a product will damage photos. If a product passes the P.A.T., it is safe to use with your photos.

photo corners   Paper with adhesive on the back used to adhere photos to a page on the corners. Used to adhere photos in scrapbooks and photo albums without applying adhesive directly to the photo.

photo display album   A combination of special scrapbook pages along with photos displayed in regular sheet protectors.

photo pool   The selection of pictures available to choose from.

picture pebbles   Smooth, flat, clear-colored pebbles. Use these to place over words to give them an enlarged or distorted look.

polypropylene, polyethylene, and **polyester**   Stable plastics that are safe for photos.

post-bound albums   Albums that are held together with metal posts that run through the pages.

pre-embossed paper   Paper with a raised design. Some of it is thick, like cardstock, and some is vellum.

primary colors   Red, yellow, and blue. These are the base from which all other colors are created.

product swap   A scrapbookers' swap meet where the host gathers up duplicates of products or tools that she doesn't use anymore and calls up some friends. They bring their unwanted scrapbooking items to trade. After it's done, you've got a clean closet and tons of new products to put in it.

punch   (1) A tool used to create small shapes. (2) The shapes created by the punches.

puzzle templates   Templates in puzzle shapes.

PVC (Polyvinyl Chlorides)   Because this substance is harmful to photos, scrapbookers should avoid it and use products that are composed of polypropylene.

Quilling   The art of rolling paper strips into different formations such as flowers and shapes.

red-eye pen   Used to take the "red eye" out of flash photographs.

reversible adhesive   An adhesive that can be undone.

rubber stamp   A detailed, intricate design cut out of rubber and mounted on wood or foam. A design is made by applying color to the rubber and imprinting that on paper.

scrapbook   An artfully arranged collection of photographs, memorabilia, and journaling that's fun to look at.

scrapbooking club   A group of scrapbookers that meet regularly to encourage each other and compare books.

scrapbooking magazine   A magazine devoted to scrapbooking, featuring layout ideas, product uses, and purchasing information.

scroll and brush pens   Pens that have one tip for coloring and one for writing.

secondary colors   Colors created by blending primary colors. Orange, green, and violet are the secondary colors created by mixing combinations of red, yellow, and blue.

serendipity squares   Small collage pieces that have been created by randomly gluing scraps on a large sheet of paper then cutting the large collaged piece into squares.

shade   A color with black added to it.

shaker box   A 3-D accent made by creating two hollow square frames and gluing them on top of each other with decorative accents in the middle that shake around.

shape cutters   Tools designed to cut shapes, such as ovals and circles. The cutters can be adjusted to create different sizes of these shapes.

simple scrapbook   An album devoted to a nonevent theme instead of a traditional chronological event–oriented album.

specialty paper books   Books that contain information about different papers, both pattern paper and plain. Some may come with extras, such as templates.

specialty templates   Cut-out shapes that match a theme.

specific pattern paper   Pattern paper with a themed pattern, such as weddings, vacations, or holidays.

spiral-bound books   Albums that are secured with a metal or plastic spiral binding running up the side.

stationery   Paper with a decorative border that is blank on the inside.

sticker   An adhesive decorative accent ranging in size from a few centimeters across to a full page.

strap-binding albums   Albums secured with plastic straps that run through a holder directly on the pages to keep the book in place.

tape roller   A device that distributes tape on the back of photos and scrapbooking pages.

template   A stencil used to trace shapes onto scrapbook pages or photos.

tertiary colors   Also called intermediate colors, these are blends of primary and secondary colors. Colors like red-orange and blue-green are tertiary colors.

theme   The overall emphasis of a page or scrapbook.

theme album   A scrapbook devoted to one idea. Some popular theme albums focus on birthdays, weddings, and school days.

three-ring binders   Albums with three metal rings of varying sizes to attach the album covers and hold pages.

time capsule   A container holding historical records or objects that represent a culture and that is deposited for preservation.

tint   A color that has had white mixed in.

title sheets   Pages with a variety of pre-made titles. They are often used as the starting point for a section in a scrapbook.

tole painting   Painting on wood, typically done in a rustic style and depicting country scenes.

triad   A group of three colors that form a triangle on the color wheel.

vellum   A lightweight, translucent paper.

velveteen   An archival paper with a fabric-like, velvety texture.

vivelle   An archival paper with a fabric-like texture similar to a terry cloth towel.

wax, or grease, pencils   Soft pencils designed for use on photographs.

wide-edge scissors   Decorative-edge scissors that make a cut that is five times deeper than normal scissors.

workshop   A class usually held at a scrapbooking store and taught by an expert. Participants bring photos and pages to work on and get advice from the instructor.

xyron machine   A machine that applies adhesive to pages and can also laminate.

Index